THE CAREER CHANGE QUEST

How To Unstuck, Change or Kick-Start Your Career and Finally Do What You Really Want to Do

ELBERT HOLDEN

© Copyright 2021 Elbert Holden - All rights reserved.

The content contained within this book may not be reproduced, duplicated or transmitted without direct written permission from the author or the publisher.

Under no circumstances will any blame or legal responsibility be held against the publisher, or author, for any damages, reparation, or monetary loss due to the information contained within this book. Either directly or indirectly. You are responsible for your own choices, actions, and results.

Legal Notice:

This book is copyright protected. This book is only for personal use. You cannot amend, distribute, sell, use, quote or paraphrase any part, or the content within this book, without the consent of the author or publisher.

Disclaimer Notice:

Please note the information contained within this document is for educational and entertainment purposes only. All effort has been executed to present accurate, up to date, and reliable, complete information. No warranties of any kind are declared or implied. Readers acknowledge that the author is not engaging in the rendering of legal, financial, medical or professional advice. The content within this book has been derived from various sources. Please consult a licensed professional before attempting any techniques outlined in this book.

By reading this document, the reader agrees that under no circumstances is the author responsible for any losses, direct or indirect, which are incurred as a result of the use of the information contained within this document, including, but not limited to, — errors, omissions, or inaccuracies.

About the Author

I am a Career Counselor/Advisor by profession. I have a bachelor's degree in psychology and a master's degree in counseling. Practically, I have been working in this field for seven years. As a career counselor/advisor, I assist clients in assessing their interests, personalities, and abilities to choose and pursue the profession that best matches them. I advise folks who haven't decided on a career path or are unsatisfied with their current one. I spend most of my day as a career counselor interacting with clients. Early sessions should focus on the client's background and conduct to assist them in better understanding their own motives and desires. With a broad range of experience, it's easy for me to guide a client through the process of researching fields that match their interests, conducting informational interviews with them to supplement their research, and finally targeting or creating specific job positions that meet their needs. I address almost every problem one can probably face related to their careers.

SPECIAL BONUS!

Want this bonus book for **FREE?**

Get **FREE**, unlimited access to it and all of my new books by joining the Fan Base!

SCAN/W YOUR CAMERA TO JOIN!

Table of Contents

INTRODUCTION 1

CHAPTER 1: KNOWING YOURSELF 6

CHAPTER 2: THE ULTIMATE FRAMEWORK FOR A SUCCESSFUL CAREER 34

CHAPTER 3: THIRTEEN FIELDS TO EXPLORE FOR YOUR CAREER 60

CHAPTER 4: SEARCHING, INTERVIEWING AND GETTING HIRED 83

CHAPTER 5: IF THEY CAN DO IT, WHY CAN'T YOU? 107

CHAPTER 6: THE FUTURE OF WORK 125

CHAPTER 7: EDUCATION, EXPERIENCE AND CREDIBILITY 142

CHAPTER 8: FOR THE ENTREPENEURIAL MINDED 159

CHAPTER 9: START YOUR BUSINESS IN 2021 183

CONCLUSION 199

REFERENCES 200

INTRODUCTION

Do you have a passion but are unsure how to turn it into a career? Do you want to make a career change but aren't sure where to begin? Are you concerned about your career advancement? Or do you sometimes feel like drowning in a sea of information because you've received so much advice? You're not the only person to feel this way!

Here's where you'll find your ideal career! This detailed and revised new edition features over 400 cool professions, ranging from social media and IT to employment in design, hospitality, medicine, technology, law, and the environment.

If you're a seasoned professional who is desperately looking for a change or a newcomer who's about to start in the workforce, you want to make the best decisions possible right away. If you wish the work to be more of a dance than a drag, this book will expertly guide and mentor you through the process of creating a career you'll enjoy, no matter where you are on your journey.

SUCCEED in the right career instead of settling! Are you working in a job that you don't enjoy? Are you in the wrong line of work? Is there an industry that isn't a good fit for you? Unstuck yourself! Find a new job that you are genuinely passionate about. This book will assist you in realizing your dream.

The book outlines tried-and-true methods for getting where you want to go. The primary step, to begin with, is to accept that the traditional job-search rules and procedures will not work for you. Standard applicants were in mind when resumes and job boards were created. As a career changer, you must go above and beyond the basics, using specifically tailored strategies to make your candidacy stand out. The book teaches you how to:

- Understand hiring managers' concerns — and act like them.
- Make a resume that grabs the attention of employers.
- Highlight transferable skills that employers are looking for.
- Rebrand yourself - Rebranding is the process of aligning your professional identity with your current goals
- Recruit "ambassadors" from your network to reach decision-makers.
- Interviews are easier to ace if you know how to use difficult questions to your benefit.
- Persuade skeptic bosses to put their prejudices aside and take a gamble on you.
- Negotiate a fair wage and benefits package, even though you're a "newcomer" to the industry.

Career changers face specific obstacles that necessitate new approaches.

This book includes invaluable tips and diagnostic resources to assist you in deciding on a new profession—or a career shift within your current sector. It's also useful for people who don't know what they want to do "when they grow up."

This book promises you to find the easiest and the most beneficial ways to choose the best career, as per your interest. It includes various practical strategies that will solve all the problems that are causing hindrance in getting your desired job. Whether you are a fresh graduate or a professional person who feels that the current position is not what they want and is looking for something that meets their interests, this book is a complete solution.

Cut the fat from your work quest and find something you enjoy. You'll learn how to make yourself stand out to recruiters and employers in this job-hunting and career-change guide. This guide will provide you listing "Dream Job" as your current role on your resume, with directions to figuring out what you want out of work and how to answer those tricky interview questions with finesse. Get a leg up on your desired job search or a leg up on changing occupations.

Elbert Holden

The strategies in this guide have been tried and proven by job seekers and newcomers to the market, including myself. Everyone who has heard them from me has expressed gratitude, stating that the tactics have been extremely beneficial to them.

People who have been fired, laid off, or thrown out of a job will find remedies in this book. Perhaps they've grown dissatisfied of their current position and wish to move on. Even if you have no experience, this book will show you how to acquire a job and be employed at your desired occupation.

The author and job seekers worldwide have used the tactics, tips, and techniques offered in this book to find work, including in countries where the unemployment rate was over 70%. The methods taught in this book will work for you no matter where you live.

Do you understand why finding jobs and career prospects in this economy has been so challenging for you in your online job search? Why have other job seekers been able to get work more quickly than you?

You will be able to master each of the following skills in this book and land the work you deserve:

- Gain the courage to apply for the job you want.
- How to Write a Strong Resume.

- Learn Novel Approaches to Getting Selected, Your Resume Selected and Interviewed.
- How to Tell Your Prospective Employer What You Have to Offer Effectively.
- How to Conduct a Successful Phone or In-Person Interview.
- How to Survive an Interview Without Being Nervous or Afraid.
- The Three Most Effective Job Application Methods.
- How to Apply for and Get the Job You Want Using social media.
- How to Apply the Law of Averages to Job Search.
- How to Be in the Right Mindset for Applying for and Getting the Job You Want.

CHAPTER 1

KNOWING YOURSELF

Sometimes it takes our whole life for us to figure out what we have always wanted from our lives because we hardly pay attention to knowing ourselves. This chapter holds the secrets that will help you understand yourself and make you realize its importance in our practical life.

What are your values, and how do we define them?

Personal values are the qualities and behaviors that inspire us and direct our decisions. Perhaps you place a high value on authenticity. You believe in being truthful wherever possible, and you believe it is important to say what you really believe. You are likely to be disappointed in yourself if you do not speak your mind. Perhaps you place a high value on kindness. You leap at the opportunity to support others and are generous with your time and money when it comes to charitable organizations or friends and family.

Those are only two examples of personal beliefs. Each has its own set of values, which can be very different from one another. Some people like to compete, while others prefer to work together. Some people seek excitement, while others seek protection. Values are important because they affect how you feel. If you live according to your values, you will feel better; if you don't, you will feel worse. This is true for both daily decisions and broader life decisions.

For example, if you enjoy adventure, allowing yourself to be coerced by parents or others into making "healthy" choices like a secure office job and a settled home life would likely make you feel suffocated. On the other hand, a profession that includes travel, starting your own company, or other risk and adventure opportunities might be more suitable for you.

If you value protection, on the other hand, the opposite is true. What some may consider a "dream" opportunity to travel the world and be your own boss may leave you feeling insecure and yearning for a more stable life. Your values are the things that are vital to you in your daily life and work. They (should) decide your goals, and they're probably the indicators you use to determine whether or not your life is going the way you want it to. Life is generally nice – you're happy and content – when the things you do and the way you act fit your beliefs. When these don't fit with your own beliefs, however, things start to feel off. This can be a major source of dissatisfaction. This is why it's important to make a deliberate effort to define your beliefs.

Everyone is unique, and what makes one person happy can make another feel nervous or uninterested. Defining and living by your personal values will help you feel more satisfied and make decisions that provide you happiness, even if they don't make sense to others. In the parts that follow, you'll learn how to do so.

Identifying and Defining Values

You get to know what is really important to you as you establish your personal values. Looking back on your life and identifying times when you felt very comfortable and happy that you were making good decisions is a good place to start.

<u>Step 1:</u> Make a list of your best moments.
Use examples from your professional and personal lives. This will ensure that your responses are balanced.

- So, what were you up to?
- Did others accompany you? Who is it, exactly?
- What other factors contributed to your contentment?

<u>Step 2:</u> Think of the moments when you were proudest of yourself. Make use of examples from your professional and personal lives.

- Why were you so pleased with yourself?
- Did other people admire you as much as you did? Who is it, exactly?
- What other factors played a role in your sense of pride?

Step 3: Make a list of the moments when you felt the most fulfilled and pleased.

Using both professional and personal examples this time.

- What's needed or not needed?
- What made the experience meaningful in your life, and how did it do so?
- What other aspects of your life led to your sense of fulfillment?

Step 4: Based on your feelings of satisfaction, pride, and fulfillment, determine your top values.

Why is it that each encounter is so significant and memorable? To get started, look through the list of popular personal values below, and aim for around ten top values. (As you go through the list, you can notice that some of these overlap.) For example, if you value philanthropy, culture, and kindness, one of your top values may be service to others.

Compassion	Altruism	Ambition	Perfection	Assertiveness
Honesty	focus	Excellence	Adventurousness	Accountability
Intelligence	Commitment	Generosity	Self-control	Humility
Curiosity	Cooperation	Creativity	Decisiveness	Service
Discipline	Independence	Fairness	Positivity	Stability
Simplicity	Discretion	Empathy	Leadership	Dynamism
Competitiveness	Elegance	Sensitivity	Speed	Vitality
Devoutness	Control	Serenity	Faith	Structure

Step 5: Make a list of the most important beliefs.

This is possibly the most difficult move because it requires you to look deep inside yourself. It's also the most critical move because you'll have to choose between options that meet different values when deciding. You must decide which value is more valuable to you at this stage.

Make a list of your top values in no particular order. Examine the first two principles and ask yourself, "Which of these would I prefer if I could only fulfil one of them?" Visualize yourself in a position where you'd have to make the decision. Consider the following scenario: you must choose between selling your house and moving to another country to do important humanitarian aid work or keeping your house and volunteering to do charity work closer to home. Continue working your way through the list, comparing each value to the next until you have it in the correct order.

Step 6: Reiterate the core principles.
Examine the highest-priority ideals to ensure that they are consistent with your life and vision for yourself.
- Do you feel confident about yourself because of these values?
- Are your top three principles something you're proud of?
- Will you be relaxed and proud to tell people you love and admire your values?
- Do these ideas reflect things you'd support, even if your option isn't common and you're in the minority?

When you consider your principles when making choices, you can be certain that you can maintain your sense of honesty and do what you believe is right and make decisions with trust and consistency. You'll also know that what you're doing is best for your happiness and fulfillment now and in the future.

Making value-based decisions isn't always easy. Making a decision that you know is right is, on the other hand, a lot easier in the long run.

How to Change Your Values When Needed

Your personal beliefs don't have to be rigid. Although some of your core values are likely to remain constant throughout your life, others will shift as per the change in your circumstances or as you grow older and develop a different perspective on what matters. Even if the values remain constant, the order in which they are prioritized can change.

Starting a family and caring for children, for example, may cause you to place a higher value on the protection and financial stability than you did when you were single. A divorce can also rekindle a desire for independence and self-discovery. As a result, it's important to check in regularly to see if your values have shifted. If your results are different, repeat the brainstorming, listing, and prioritizing process.

How much should this be done? At least once in a year, and every time you experience a major life change such as a work loss, grief, death, divorce, or other major life change, it is usually a good idea. Of course, you'll want to keep reading and returning to your values on a far more frequent basis than once a year, and if anything doesn't feel right any longer, feel free to rewrite your values right away. Re-examine your priorities and rewrite them where appropriate to represent your current or newly prioritized values after you've made your new list.

How to discover your passion

The process of finding your passion might not be as easy as it seems, but it is well worth the effort. You should start searching for a new career if you hate going to work, are you chronically lacking motivation, or find what you're doing boring and repetitive? Staying in your current job will not only keep you trapped and depressed, but it will also restrict you from reaching your full potential in life.

Instead, imagine this:

You get out of bed early in the morning, eager to get to work. You can work longer hours than the average person, but you don't find it challenging because your work hours fly by. You are always in a state of mind known as "flow," in which you lose track of time and the outside world, completely immersed in the task at hand. A Job isn't what many people think about when they think of work; it's something enjoyable, interesting, and exciting.

If you have a career or a job that you dislike or even despise, this would seem like a pipe dream. And such a thing would never be possible if you never put in the effort to discover what you are passionate about. It is, however, not only a possibility but a likelihood; if you dare to inquire, "How do I find my passion?" imagine the possibilities and look for what you love.

Listed below are a few things that will help you in learning more about how to discover your passion:

1. Do you already have a passion for something?

Do you have a hobby or a pastime that you enjoyed as a kid but never considered as a career option? There's definitely a way for you to make a living doing something you like, whether it's reading comic books, collecting something, or designing or constructing something. Open a comic book store or an online comic book site. You're already ahead of the curve if you have a passion for something. Now all you got to do is look at how you can profit from it

2. Figure out what you spend hours reading about.

When I get excited about something, I'll read about it for hours. I'll go out and buy some books and magazines. I'll spend days searching the web for more details. There could be a few options here for you, and they're all viable career paths. Don't shut your mind off to these ideas. Examine them until you're satisfied, and this will assist you in getting started as you learn how to find your passion.

3. Have a brainstorming session

If you're wondering how to find my passion and nothing comes to mind right away, take out a paper and pen and start listing down ideas. This doesn't need to be a well-organized list. It may simply be a piece of paper with scribbles or doodles on it. All of this will come in handy at some point. Look for ideas around your home, on your tablet, or on your bookshelf, and write down everything that comes to mind. At this stage, there are no ideas that can be considered as bad ideas.

4. Consult with others

There are always some people in your life that you respect, and there are aspects of their personalities that you wish to emulate. If at all necessary, approach them and pick their brain. Analyze carefully how they got to where they are now and if they believe they've found their calling. The more options you discover, the more likely you will learn how to discover your passion in the long run. This may mean that you spend your free time talking to friends and family, colleagues, or even strangers.

5. Hold off on quitting your job just yet.

Don't just hand in your resignation tomorrow if you find your calling, your passion. It's best to keep your current work while you investigate your options. It's even better if you can do your passion as a side job and earn money for a few months or a year. It allows you to save money (which you'll need if you go into business for yourself) while also allowing you to practice the skills you'll need.

6. First, give it a shot.

When you're trying to discover how to find your passion, it's best to put your new idea to the test before committing to it as a career. At first, do it as a hobby or a side job to see if it's really your true calling.

You can be passionate about it for a few days, but if you are passionate about it for at least a few months, it is where the rubber meets the road. You've probably found it if you pass this exam.

7. Do as much thorough research as possible

Learn as much as you can about your passion. You could have already been doing this if this has been a long-time hobby of yours. In either case, conduct the additional study. Read any website you can find on the subject and invest in the best books available. Find other people who do what you want to do for a living in your area or on the Internet and question them about it.

How much do they get, and what kind of education and training did they require? What abilities are needed, and how did they develop? What suggestions do they have for you?

You'll most frequently find out that people are eager to provide advice.

8. Practice, practice, practice, and then practice some more.

If you're close to figuring out your passion, don't go into it with a beginner's skill set. You must have technical skills if you want to make money — to be a professional. Get very good at your future job, and you'll be able to make a lot of money. Train for hours on end and learn to concentrate; if it's something you like; the practice can be enjoyable.

9. Never Give Up Trying

It's true that you won't find your passion right away. You will, however, fail if you give up after a few days. Keep searching, even if it takes months, and you'll eventually find it. Maybe you thought you'd discovered your calling, only to find after a few months that it wasn't for you. Restart your quest for a new passion. There's a good chance you'll have more than one passion in your lifetime, so take advantage of them all.

Have you discovered your calling but haven't been able to make a living from it? Continue to try and try before you succeed. Giving up too soon is a sure way to fail because success does not come easily. Remember that this will take a lot of time and effort, but it will be the greatest investment you've ever made. If you take out and invest the time to learn how to find your passion, you will find that your days are more rewarding and that you are happier and more well-adjusted in the long run.

Why is being passionate about a role important?

Every person will have two choices in front of them during the early stages of their job search, from which they must choose one. Money or passion are the two choices. Let's face it, a person is very rarely blessed with the option of both.

If you choose money, you will not be able to find fulfillment in your work but will be able to earn well, while if you choose to love, you will be able to be happy at work while also earning well. It is assumed that everyone possesses a unique talent, which some discover in their early years of existence and others do not. Though there's nothing wrong with working for a living, we can at least strive to discover our natural talents and passions.

How to Discover Yourself

The ability to fully understand yourself is the most valuable skill you can have. Instead of seeking permission from someone to do what you already know you can do, you know what you need to do when you know who you are. It helps you avoid a lot of the stress from wasting time on the wrong stuff. Yes, trial and errors are a part of life, but this allows you to identify the best places to experiment in the first place. You will gain trust, appreciate your meaning, and begin to have a greater effect on the world once you have a complete and better understanding of yourself.

So, how do you figure out who you are and what you can do with your life? The following are the six steps you must take to discover your true self:

1. **Be quiet.**

You can't and won't know yourself unless and until you take the time to be still. Many people are unacquainted with themselves because silence terrifies them; being alone with all of their flaws looking back at them is too awkward. But you won't be able to see every aspect of your life — the good and the bad — until you get alone, assess yourself, and be honest with yourself. Quiet yourself, and you will find your true self.

1. Recognize who you are rather than who you want to be.

I know you have a clear vision of who you want to be, but it may not be who you were created to be; this is why understanding who you really are is so critical. When you understand who you are, you'll be able to see how you and your unique talents fit into the larger picture.

And, though there are several points in your path to help you discover yourself, taking a personality test and the StrengthsFinder test is the best place to start. (If it has been five years or more since you did one of these, you can retake them.) No, these self-evaluations aren't accurate, but they do help you reflect on the difference you're meant to make in the world by identifying your top areas of power.

3. Figure out what you're good at (and not good at).

This is the most difficult and demanding step in the process of discovering who you are, but it is also the most important. Sure, it takes trial and error to figure out what you're really good at, and no, I don't want you to quit before you've given it your all, but knowing when to stop is a skill that everyone can master.

When you've put in enough time, and your efforts aren't paying off, leave. How much time is enough? You are the only one that can make the decision. But quitting correctly isn't about giving up; it's about making space for something better. When your acts exhaust you rather than igniting your enthusiasm and inspiring you to do more, it's time to shift your attention. Your abilities will reveal who you are.

4. Figure out what you're really interested in.

Following a passion of some sort is a positive thing, and you should pay attention to it when it appears because it means an area of your life that you should focus on more. It's a positive thing if we're talking about pursuing your passion at work. And it's a positive thing if we're talking about getting more life love. You'll have a greater effect if you focus more on your passions and gain a deeper understanding of yourself. Passion fuels effort, and consistent effort yields performance.

5. Request feedback.

Hearing what people have to say about you can be beneficial if you don't know yourself. Ask them two basic questions: "What strengths do you think I should work on more?" and "What do you think my weaknesses are that I can focus on?" Of course, their feedback isn't always perfect and right, but it will most likely point out a few places that you can look at again. This move is significant for those who are having trouble figuring out who they are. Those closest to us may be able to see something in us that we cannot see in ourselves.

6. Take a close look at your relationships.

Your relationships are a big part of getting to know yourself. The significance of understanding yourself becomes even more evident as you remember that you'll never really know someone else until you discover yourself. This is certainly true for business leaders because you would be lost as a leader if you do not know the people on your team. This law, however, extends to every relationship you have in your life. Just as much as you need to know yourself, some people need to know who you are. People require you — the genuine you.

Use your thoughts to overcome your greatest fears, and once you know who you are supposed to be, your goal will eventually outweigh your fears. You will invest less time spinning your wheels until you understand who you are. Concentrating on your strengths will give you the traction you need to start making a bigger and better impact in the world. When you know who you are, you will have more peace and achieve success faster than ever before.

The Flower Exercise

The flower exercise is a self-evaluation tool that will help you learn more about yourself, your talents, abilities, and interests. This exercise is very useful in determining your work goals and decisions because the secret to finding your ideal job is to discover who you are. In a nutshell, the flower exercise aids you in determining what style of job is best for you. It contains a series of questions to help you figure out exactly what you're looking for. These inquiries are shaped like petals on a flower. Each petal reflects a different part of your dream job that you should think about.

There are seven petals on the flower. The seven petals, each of which explain who you are and what kind of profession or work is best for you, are as follows:

- Petal 1: Preferred Living and Working Location
- Petal 2: Salary Range and Role Preferences
- 3rd Petal: Favorite Working Environment
- Petal 4: Job Objectives and Hobbies
- Petal 5: Favorite People to Work With
- Petal 6: Favorite Fields or Sectors of Special Knowledge
- Petal 7: Skills That Can Be Transferred

Each petal guides you and helps you organize your thoughts about your ideal job by asking you to write down the answers to hypothetical questions. This activity will assist job seekers, and career changers (you) define who you are and what you want to achieve out of your professional life.

Let us now discuss it in a bit more detail.

1) Geography

What city would you like to live in? Please list the top three factors that best define the location of your ideal job.

- Do you prefer the climate of cold or the heat?
- Is it better to reside in a big city or a small town?
- Are you near a beach, a forest, or a mountain?
- What are your ideal cities and countries to work in?

2) Position and Salary/Compensation

Please answer the following questions as descriptively as possible:

- What is the ideal wage and level of obligation for you?
- Which role would you like to begin? What is the title of your position?
- What is your level of accountability?
- Annual salary target: £, $, or your local currency
- Monthly wage goal: Considering your salary will assist you in negotiating a salary. It will also motivate you to look for new opportunities and options, such as diversifying your income streams, passive income, and so on.

3) Favorite Working Conditions

What are the best working conditions for you? Please choose your top 3-4 priorities and write them down.

- Do you want to start a small company or work for a big corporation?
- Do you want a 9-to-5 career or one with more flexibility?
- Is it better to be inside or outside?
- Do you prefer to stay in one location or fly extensively?
- A job that is prescribed or work that is spontaneous?
- Do you prefer working alone or in a supportive group?
- More freedom or more structure?
- What are the ideal working conditions for producing the most successful results?

4) Work Goals and Interests

In this portion, you'll consider your most important professional goals and interests. What is your life's objective, intent, calling, or mission? You'll attempt to answer this question on your own terms. You should consider your moral compass and spiritual ideals as guiding principles.

Please also choose the top three and rate them:

- **Working with the human mind**: bringing more wisdom, reality, and clarity into the world.

- **Working with the human body**: providing shelter, food, clothes, fitness, or health.
- **Working with the senses**: bringing more beauty into the world through art, music, flowers, photography, decoration, crafts, jewelry, and paintings.
- **Working with the human conscience:** To bring justice, morality, righteousness, and integrity to the world.
- **Working with the human heart**: To bring more compassion and empathy to the world.
- **Working with the Environment** - To ensure the planet's long-term viability and protection.

5) Favorite People

What types of people do you prefer to collaborate with? This query will also assist you in determining the type of organizational culture and atmosphere in which you wish to work. Do you want to be occupied by people who are highly ambitious and competitive? Do you want to be a part of a multicultural team? Make a bullet-point list of your preferences to help you remember them.

6) Subject-Matter Expertise or Industry Sectors

What are some of your favorite fields of expertise or interests? This section allows you to choose the top markets, industries, and fields in which you are interested and knowledgeable. How well-versed are you in these fields? What are your strategies for moving forward and learning more? Make a list of all of these fields and subjects. Take notes on your current knowledge as well as your plans for future learning and growth.

7) Skills That Can Be Transferred

Some of your transferable skills are your favorites? Consider the skills you enjoy using the most. Make a list of your technical and personal skills, and write them down. Consider your life experiences or stories in which you have felt competent and accomplished. When was the last time when you felt really satisfied and productive? So, what were you up to? What skills did you use during these encounters? Make a list of these stories, memories, and abilities.

When you're finished with this exercise, pay attention to your gut feelings and emotions. Make it useful, enjoyable, and interesting to you. As required, adapt and customize it. Even if you only have 15 minutes, you can complete this exercise and learn a lot about your ideal career.

As you complete this exercise, you will come up with your own interpretation and plot.

Identifying what you're good at by conducting a SWOT analysis.

A SWOT (strengths, weaknesses, opportunities, and threats) analysis is a popular technical method for evaluating a company's history, current, and potential role. It gives corporate leaders a fresh perspective on what the company does well, where the company's problems are, and which paths to take.

A personal SWOT analysis will help anyone achieve their career goals in the same way. It gives you insights into your personality's strengths and weaknesses, the obstacles you face, and the prospects that are available to you now and in the future.

Strengths and opportunities are things you consider positive and, in your hands, while weaknesses and challenges are negative and determined by outside factors. You will use this information to investigate the relationship between your strengths and weaknesses and how to use your strengths to maximize opportunities and strengthen your weaknesses to minimize risks.

Personality types

The most crucial element to select what fits your personality is knowing your persona. These are the 16 personality types on the Myers-Briggs Personality Indicator (MBTI). I have briefly presented each one so that you can understand what personality you hold:

ISTJ: THE INSPECTOR (Introverted, Sensing, Thinking, Judging)
The four-letter code ISTJ (introversion, sensing, thinking, judgment). The ISTJ personality style is reserved, sensible, and quiet by nature.

ISTP: THE CRAFTER (Introverted, Sensing, Thinking, Perceiving)
People with ISTP personalities value their alone time and are intensely self-reliant. Action, new experiences, hands-on tasks, and the ability to work at their own pace are all favorites of ISTPs.

ISFJ: THE PROTECTOR (Introverted, Sensing, Feeling, Judging)
The Protector personality type (introverted, sensing, feeling, judging is known for being reserved, warm-hearted, and responsible.

ISFP: THE ARTIST (Introverted, Sensing, Feeling, Perceiving)
Quiet, easygoing, and peaceful are common characteristics of ISFP personalities.

INFJ: THE ADVOCATE (Introverted, Intuitive, Feeling, Judging)
People with INFJ personalities are imaginative, gentle, and compassionate and are often referred to as "Advocates" or "Idealists."

INFP: THE MEDIATOR (Introverted, Intuitive, Feeling, Perceiving)
The INFP personality type is sometimes referred to as an "idealist" or "mediator." Introverted, idealistic, imaginative, and motivated by

high values, people with this personality type are common. INFPs are very passionate about making the planet a better place.

INTJ: THE ARCHITECT (Introverted, Intuitive, Thinking, Judging)

People with INTJ personalities are highly analytical, imaginative, and logical and are often referred to as "Architects" or "Strategists."

INTP: THE THINKER (Introverted, Intuitive, Thinking, Perceiving)

INTP personality types are often characterized as quiet and analytical. Such people love being alone, contemplating how things work, and devising solutions to problems. They have a rich inner universe and prefer to concentrate on their own feelings rather than the outside world. They usually do not have a large social circle, but they have a small circle of friends.

ESTP: THE PERSUADER (Extraverted, Sensing, Thinking, Perceiving)

Outgoing, action-oriented, and dramatic are prominent characteristics of people with this personality style. They are outgoing people who love socializing with a diverse group of people. They are more content with the present than with the future, and they are observed to focus on facts rather than indulging in a broader view of things and circumstances.

ESTJ: THE DIRECTOR (Extraverted, Sensing, Thinking, Judging)

Such personalities are often characterized as rational, commanding individuals. They are assertive and focused on making sure that everything runs smoothly and according to the rules. Tradition, standards, and laws are essential to them. They have clear convictions and sound judgment, and they expect others to act in accordance with these values.

ESFP: THE PERFORMER (Extraverted, Sensing, Feeling, Perceiving)

People with the ESFP personality style are known for being outgoing, resourceful, and spontaneous. People with this personality type enjoy being the center of attention and are often referred to as "class clowns" or "entertainers."

ESFJ: THE CAREGIVER (Extraverted, Sensing, Feeling, Judging)

The ESFJ personality style is known for being outgoing, trustworthy, coordinated, and tender-hearted. Interacting with other people gives ESFJs energy. They are usually characterized as gregarious and outgoing.

ENFP: THE CHAMPION (Extraverted, Intuitive, Feeling, Perceiving)

This personality style is charismatic, enthusiastic, and self-sufficient. They are inventive and creative people who thrive in environments that enable them to do so. ENFPs make up about 5% to 7% of the population.

ENFJ: THE GIVER (Extraverted, Intuitive, Feeling, Judging)

ESFJ, ENFP, INFP, ISFJ, and INTP are acronyms for several other groups. Warmth, outgoingness, loyalty, and sensitivity are all traits associated with the ENFJ personality style.

ENTP: THE DEBATER (Extraverted, Intuitive, Thinking, Perceiving)

This personality TYPE is known for being creative, intelligent, and expressive. They are also known for their idea-oriented nature, which is why they've been dubbed "the innovator," "the visionary," and "the debater."

ENTJ: THE COMMANDER (Extraverted, Intuitive, Thinking, Judging)

The Myers-Briggs Type Indicator identifies 16 personality groups, and the acronym ENTJ stands for one of them. Isabel Myers and her mother, Katherine Briggs, developed this well-known personality test. The questionnaire is based on Carl Jung's personality trait theory. People with this personality style are also described as assertive, optimistic, and outspoken by others

Why is Career Reinvention so difficult?

Many historically useful work-related skills are quickly becoming redundant at a time when tech advances and exogenous events like the COVID pandemic are transforming industries and employment, as well as the very essence of how work is done. Traditional ways of doing things are giving way to new ways of doing things. And, in a world where COVID has increased the speed of imaginative disruption, it's difficult to overstate the extent of work displacement.

Many people, especially those in their forties and fifties, have trouble imagining how to remake their lives. For millions of people, career reinvention is more than just a nice-sounding concept.

It may seem that remaking a career is both complicated and frightening. It shouldn't be that way, though. The simple fact is that it is only viewed as daunting because most people have no idea how to change professions. People are put off by the "I don't know how" syndrome. The most difficult thing is getting over it.

People are conditioned to work within their skill sets and training in jobs that they are familiar with. They feel secure and safe in the surroundings they are familiar with, and leaving it is, well, unsettling. As a result, the transition is regarded as difficult.

Many people are still hesitant to reinvent themselves because they are afraid of failing. However, this is an unfounded fear. Is there anything worthwhile that has ever been done without taking a chance? In the face of inflation or obsolescence, doing nothing is insane.

When we are used to a career and a paycheck, it isn't easy to reinvent ourselves. We can be lulled into a wrong sense of financial stability, leading to laziness and procrastination in coping with the inevitable. We don't take action before we lose our jobs and get the proverbial kick in the buttocks.

Rather than reacting, take the initiative to make a change. It's time to make a career change whether you're stuck in a rut or your skills are on the verge of being obsolete.

To be sure, reinvention necessitates a lot of effort, but it becomes more manageable when broken down into sequential measures, just like every other issue.

CHAPTER 2

THE ULTIMATE FRAMEWORK FOR A SUCCESSFUL CAREER

This chapter provides you an in-depth understanding of the ultimate framework for successful career changes.

Top 10 reasons as to why you would possibly want to change your career

Switching or changing your career can be one of the most challenging experiences you'll have in your career. You may have worked for a company for a long time and have become a part of its culture. Routines, habits, and small everyday activities, such as when and where you take coffee breaks. leaving that sort of familiar atmosphere behind can be terrifying for even the most experienced worker. Then there's the matter of personal ties. In case you work at an office, your coworkers have almost certainly become colleagues — or at least comfortable acquaintances. When you leave your job, you're saying goodbye to these people, as well as the teamwork and sense of cooperation you've built over the years.

However, in certain circumstances, a career-minded individual is forced to change jobs. Your current job may be a dead-end for your career, or you may only be able to reach your full potential in a different role. You can need to quit a job in extreme cases for your emotional well-being or protection. As painful as leaving a job can be, remaining in one can be even more so. Continue reading to discover ten of the best reasons to change career.

1. You can gain a broader base of knowledge.

Consider the learning curve you encountered when you first began your new role. There was almost certainly a time of rapid adaptation, accompanied by a longer period of learning the finer points of your work. In an ideal world, you could have completed this process by mastering your everyday tasks and becoming an expert in your department's operations. According to some studies, the average worker takes three years to master his or her particular job. The speed of industry-focused learning and skill mastery slows after that. They claim that changing jobs after the three-year period has ended resets and recharges the process, allowing you to develop and learn rapidly for another three years in the new career. While the three years aren't set in stone, it does serve as a rough roadmap and a point of comparison for evaluating what you're learning at work. Will you have to learn new skills if you move to a new job within your industry? Will those skills help you become a more well-rounded and competent professional by complementing those you already have? If that's the scenario, it might be time to start searching for a new career.

2 You can increase your earning power.

A pay raise may be difficult to ignore, and your talents could be such that you can gain significantly more by switching jobs than you are now. Not all businesses are created equal. Similarly, the same work will pay substantially different amounts in different industries. Being mindful of these inequalities — and seizing resources resulting from them — can be compelling reasons to change careers.

3. Your current job doesn't challenge you.

You've probably heard friends, acquaintances, and family members talk about having a "cushy" career, one that's simple, slow-paced, and doesn't require much effort. It seems that the perfect cushy career will be a paid nap, with only enough jobs to keep you looking busy. The truth of the workplace, on the other hand, is very different. A work that is too straightforward can be dangerous for your satisfaction and career advancement.

According to some sources, about 20% of the time, the ideal job entails truly demanding, out-of-your-comfort-zone jobs. A job that provides little to no challenging work exposes you to the various job and career-killing factors. To pass the time, you may fall into bad work habits like playing video games or surfing the Internet. Your morale will plummet, leaving you unmotivated and unable to seize opportunities as they arise. Your boss can note your boredom and interpret it as a sign that you aren't a valuable worker. It might be the time to look for a new career if you're always bored at work or don't have any problems coming across your desk. Staying challenged is important for your long-term career goals: Look for a career that allows you to do that.

4. You cannot stand your boss any longer.

Is your employer causing you to be unhappy? It's possible that you'd be better off in a different situation. Every employee is irritated by his or her employer from time to time. However, if "now and then" in your office turns into "all the time," it might be time to look for a new job. Perhaps you believe your manager isn't doing his or her job as well as you think he or she should. Perhaps you disagree with the way he or she insists on leading your squad. Perhaps you and your boss have a fundamental communication problem that makes any interaction awkward and fraught with second-guessing and mistrust. If you're in this situation, consider what it is about your boss that irritates you the most and decide if there is something you can do about it. If not, then leave.

5. Your company is about to fail or go bankrupt.

While the old adage about rats fleeing a sinking ship isn't flattering, it rings true in the workplace: if you can see that your business is on the verge of financial collapse — or worse — it's probably time to look for a new career. Companies struggle for a variety of reasons. Some could simply be in shrinking markets, where their rivals are outpacing them as their consumer base shrinks. Others lose because their representatives make bad decisions or don't understand how the economy works. In extreme situations, a leader's fraud or illegal acts could jeopardize a company, with lower-level workers bearing the brunt of the consequences if the company fails. Fortunately, all of these issues are easier to spot from inside the organization than from the outside. If you see something unusual at work, such as a large number of layoffs or regularly low quarterly revenue figures, ask your company's trusted sources questions and decide accordingly.

6. Your life has taken a significant turn.
It might be time to move on if your employer refuses to work around a big change in your life, such as the birth of a child. Let's say you marry someone who works in another state, or your spouse receives a fantastic job offer that allows you to relocate. Perhaps you're expecting a child, or a senior relative is moving in with you. You want to spend more time with your family, but your current job situation can prevent you from making that change.

Smart workers notify their employers of these life changes as soon as they occur, keeping them informed as their desires, goals, and availability alter. This practice will significantly increase your chances of adjusting your job situation to your new life situation, in addition to being a courtesy to your boss. Perhaps your boss will have enough time to adjust your work requirements or assist you in finding a new position within the business that best suits your needs. If that isn't possible, your former employer can be a valuable source of information while you look for a new career. In certain circumstances, your employer will also be willing to assist you in finding a new career, establishing a long-term partnership if you can return. If you learn that your boss doesn't value your desire for a balanced work-life balance or wants you to put your job ahead of personal and family obligations, it might be easier to bear the burden of a job change.

7. Coworkers can create a hostile environment.
Every business, workplace, and job team has its own work culture. Consider a group of baseball fans in an office where fantasy baseball is the topic of discussion in the spring, and the World Series is the topic of discussion in the fall. This type of relationship can help co-workers unite and become a stronger team, but it can also make the workplace a closed-off – and even hostile – environment for outsiders.

Consider what's at the root of your frustration if you're in a workplace where the atmosphere isn't conducive to your success, satisfaction, or comfort. Certain work environments are rigidly exclusive or focused on toxic themes, such as sexual harassment or drug and alcohol abuse. If this is the case, you can become acquainted with your state's and country's Equal Employment Opportunity (EEO) and anti-harassment rules. Via an EEO lawsuit, you might be able to put an end to a culture of illegal discrimination. However, if the issue is simply not being a part of the office community, you may decide it's best to look for a new job.

8. Your job focuses on your shortcomings.

You do not get a chance to showcase your skills? Talk to your boss; if he or she cannot assist, you will find a job that respects your abilities. Perhaps you began your current job with the expectation of applying your specific skills to meaningful work. When you first started working and learned the ins and outs of your career, you found that instead of allowing you to play to your strengths, the role required abilities, strengths, or a temperament that were not in line with who you are. Perhaps you will learn new skills that will better suit you for the role and make you happier in it. Perhaps there is a role within the organization that better suits your needs, and you can orchestrate a change. However, if the gap between what you need to do and what you want to do is wide, you may benefit from speaking with your boss.

9. You've got a better deal.

Professionals who excel in their fields are noted. After all, companies want to hire the best in their industry, and where better to look for the best than inside a competitor's upper ranks? There's a fair chance that if you do good work and are good at networking within your industry, you'll be noticed by rivals. A better deal may catch you off guard. If you're good at your current work, you're probably happy there. Another organization, on the other hand, might be willing to go to any length to entice you to join its team, including offering more money, more flexibility, or better benefits.

If a better offer comes your way, don't be afraid to ask difficult questions about the company's operations and working climate. After all, you're in charge; you could easily decline the offer and continue working in your current job.

10. You're ready to start a new job.
Your coworkers are likely to help your transition to a higher role if you've received a new degree or qualification. A change in your career goals or expectations, similar to a major life change, could necessitate you to change jobs. You may have completed a college degree that has opened new doors for you, or you may just want to change careers at this point in your life. This type of transformation usually occurs after a period of introspection, conversation at home, and preparation outside of the workplace. You may have been planning this for a long time.

If you're currently employed in a stable position, making this move can be easy. It's possible that you've formed tight bonds with your coworkers, and they're aware that your career goals are bigger than what you can achieve in your current position. Your boss may have worked with you to create a plan that allows you to return to school, and your coworkers may have been very supportive of your efforts to change your work life. Communication is the secret to making this kind of transformation successful. Don't keep it a secret if you're working on a new degree. Get your coworkers and boss used to the fact that you might be changing careers, and you might be shocked at how supportive they are when you take the plunge into the next phase of your career.

How to pick the right career path for you What is the concept of a career path?

The roles or jobs you hold as you advance in your professional life make up your career line. Your first job or college degree, for example, can direct the beginning of your professional journey. You can move or "jump vertically" into more advanced and valuable positions as your experience and skills develop. Some workers are seen to "jump laterally" into equal but separate job positions when they specialize or change career directions.

Typical career paths

Listed below are a few major examples of potential career paths in different industries:

Marketing: public relations assistant → public relations representative → assistant director of PR → director of communications

Retail: sales associate → cashier → assistant manager → store manager → regional manager

Education: teacher → curriculum coordinator → assistant principal → principal

Editorial: intern → editorial assistant → assistant editor → editor → senior editor → executive editor → editor in chief

Restaurant: dishwasher → prep cook → line cook → sous-chef → de cuisine → executive chef

Human resources: HR assistant → HR specialist → assistant director of HR → director of HR

How do you choose a career path?

Your career path should represent your aspirations, expectations for the future, and personality. These considerations will help you in selecting the best starting position and making strategic decisions over time.

As you plan your career path, keep these steps in mind:
- Create a list of your career objectives.
- Make a five- and ten-year strategy.
- Find out your personality type.
- Examine your prior knowledge.
- Examine the career criteria in relation to your qualifications.
- Examine your present skill set.
- Take note of your interests.
- Identify your core principles.
- Take into account the salary requirements.

1. Create a list of your career objectives.

Ask and answer some questions about yourself before deciding on a career path. Active contemplation assists you in narrowing down your options to something more concrete.

Consider the following questions:

- What am I looking for in a job?
- What are my guiding principles?
- What are my favorite things to do socially and in my spare time?
- What are my passions?
- What are my skills and abilities? What are my soft skills? Do I have any hard skills?
- Do I want to focus on certain technical skills or take on the responsibilities of management?

You can study future career paths better after you've answered questions like these—and any others that are important to you. It's also crucial to revisit your career goals as you develop personally and professionally to make sure they're still achievable and compatible with your passions.

2. Make a five- and ten-year strategy

Consider defining career milestones until you've narrowed down your choices. Make a list of where other people in your profession are five or ten years into their careers, as per the work titles they hold. Examine what title or advancements you want at these points in the future. Then take a glance at what you can do to achieve those objectives. You may be required to complete training programs, assume special roles, or work in a prerequisite role. You can prepare based on what improvement you can expect next year if you set career goals. Schedule time to focus on your career and aspirations daily.

3. Find out your personality type

A personality type is basically a classification of personality characteristics. There are various strategies for determining your personality type, with many of them focusing on your reactions to various situations and circumstances. Different personality types can naturally gravitate toward different interests and strengths, including occupations.

Various personality tests include a list of popular career options for each personality type. If you take several tests and one or two careers appear on several of them, that profession is worth investigating further. You can take help for this step from Chapter 1.

4. Examine your prior knowledge.

Your past job satisfaction can also influence your career choices. Recognize patterns in your previous employment, such as a preference for a particular technical ability. Analyze your previous work experience to find places where you feel satisfied.

5. Examine the career criteria in relation to your qualifications.

Many positions have basic qualification criteria for candidates and new hires, such as a high school diploma, a bachelor's degree, or a master's degree. Some roles often require candidates to have a degree in a relevant field to the position. Analyze the educational criteria for the careers you're interested in, and apply for positions that accept your current level of education, or look at getting additional degrees or certifications.

6. Examine your present skill set.

Make a list of your existing abilities, certifications, and specialties. You will also get input on your technical, interpersonal, and people management skills from peers and colleagues. This assessment will assist you in locating jobs that are a good fit for your skills.

7. Take note of your interests

You can have interests that may lead to various professions depending on your personality. Keenly examine your hobbies, volunteer opportunities, and interests to find out what you want to do. Although this information might not be relevant to your professional life, making a comprehensive list of events will help you in shortlisting your career options. If you enjoy logic puzzles, for example, you might enjoy a career in cybersecurity, or if you enjoy meeting and exploring new people, you will enjoy a traveling sales agent role. Apply for short-term jobs or volunteer opportunities to learn about new career prospects using certain experiences. This hands-on training helps you to analyze your suitability for a particular profession. Consider taking a course or certification program available for a profession that interests you if you are still in school or have a job. This experience will help you figure out whether the skills and content of the job appeal to you.

8. Identify your core principles.

Identifying your core values will assist you in focusing on a career that you enjoy. It may also assist you in identifying fields or specialty areas in which you have a strong interest. Make a list of attributes you believe an organization or its employees should possess. This list can be used to find businesses and job descriptions that share these principles.

9. Take into account the salary requirements.

Different career paths can result in a wide range of earnings. On Indeed Salaries, you can search for average salaries by job title, organization, and place. This is a good place for finding out how much money you'll make when you first start, as well as your earning potential after you've put in some time and experience. While a high salary does not always imply a fulfilling job, it is important to consider when planning your career path.

The secrets of having a satisfying and fulfilling career

What do you require to have a happy and fulfilling working life?

A few must-haves are listed below:

1. Specified boundaries

Boundaries are the invisible walls that separate you from your external structures, regulating the flow of knowledge and input between you and the outside world. You become "enmeshed" with others when your boundaries are overly hazy, making it difficult to tell where you end and others begin. You're "disengaged" when your boundaries are rigid and impenetrable, meaning you don't have a safe and reasonable relationship with others or your own life. The trick is to strike a balance – to be healthy in your interactions with others while still being secure enough in your skin, with your feelings, values, and self-worth to be able to walk through life understanding who you are and what you want, and fighting successfully for it without feeling like a constant challenge. Thinking about your life and career, ask yourself, "Am I living someone else's idea of life and success, or am I living my own?"

2. A healthy financial relationship.

If you let the money you earn rule your life, you can never be happy at work. That's what there is to it. Money can be mistaken as an energy form, and if you give it all of your power, it will drain you. On the other hand, if you can see money for what it is and concentrate on what you're really supposed to do in this world and how important you are, doors will open, and new opportunities will present themselves.

3. Dare to get away from what's exhausting you.

When your ego, fears, and dreams are all wrapped up in something, it takes bravery to say "enough of this!" People are deathly afraid of change because they've been going in a certain direction for a long time and have become overly accustomed to the result and how it should look. "Just one more year, and something has to break!" some may argue. or "This feels so wrong, but I've put money into it – I can't back out now." The problem is that no matter how much you imagine the wrong path improving, it remains wrong. It's not good for you to be doing work that drains, disappoints, and demoralizes you.

4. Gratitude and a vision of what you want to do with your life.

The more you take time to appreciate and thank what you enjoy in your life (even if it's just a sliver of your entire life experience at the moment), the more you'll be able to extend those things that bring you joy. You will become blind to the fresh and better prospects that are waiting in the wings if you never pause to feel or show appreciation for what is going well in your life and what you enjoy.

5. Willingness to put your fears in a cage.

Happiness requires versatility, transparency, and adaptability in your life. There is a minute amount of people in the world who are content to be and do the same thing every day of their lives. We mature, evolve, and grow as we get older. We yearn to stretch out, take on new adventures, spread our wings, face new challenges, and be more like who we actually want to be. All of this necessitates facing your fears. The more at ease you become with entering the cage with your fears and confronting them, the more fulfilling and stable your life and career will be.

6. A support circle that empowers you.

Finally, when it comes to early career growth, the one thing that most people overlook is other people. Many people in their era of the 20s and 30s are intensely self-focused, devoting large quantities of time and energy to acquiring more responsibility, improving their expertise, and climbing the corporate ladder. They fail to recognize that cultivating meaningful relationships with people who are encouraging, inspiring, and energizing (as well as mentoring those who are just starting) is the most effective career strategy we can devise. Developing a strong support network and community now will mean the difference between being trapped in a horrible situation for years and getting new doors open upright when you need them.

These foundations of a good and happy career will not grow independently, but they can be easily cultivated and established with dedication and concentration.

Financial impact of a Career Change

You can change careers for two reasons: job loss or dissatisfaction with the current job profile. However, quitting today and finding a wonderful opportunity tomorrow is unlikely. Changing careers necessitates a great deal of thought. It can have a significant psychological impact while also disrupting your finances.

A career change entails a loss of income, financial benefits, periods of unemployment, extra course costs, and so on. Many of such issues can be avoided with careful budgeting.

Let's look at the financial implications of changing careers and how to deal with them.

Unemployed Phase

The most significant effect of changing careers is the period of unemployment. Many people are forced to go through an interim period where they are not employed, either voluntarily or due to a lack of good choices. Without a job, you will have no money, which will significantly impact your budget. To get through this time, you should have a backup plan in places, such as an emergency fund or a sabbatical corpus.

New Certifications and Courses

A change of profession always necessitates the acquisition of new credentials or certifications. These courses will quickly deplete your savings. As a result, it is critical to research the necessary courses. Many online forums include such certifications at a low cost or even for free.

Loss of Income

You are a newcomer to the industry when you make a dramatic career change. As a result, regardless of prior experience, the new salary would be significantly lower. To offset the loss of revenue, you must prepare your finances accordingly.

Loss of Benefits

When you change jobs, you can lose certain benefits such as health care, a pension fund, travel allowances, etc. You should do extensive research on the new workplace and its benefits. As a result, you should adjust your budget to account for the new out-of-pocket costs.

Implications On Household Finances

When it comes to changing jobs, the household budget has the greatest impact. Any rise in or loss of income can have a significant impact on your family's budget. Prepare for the adjustments ahead of time. To reduce the financial effect of a career change, talk to your family, adjust your expenses and savings, and make a gradual move.

You must take a comprehensive inventory of your existing savings and spending. This will assist you in developing a strategy for dealing with the financial consequences of changing careers.

What is a successful career and how do we have one?

The process of a successful career is described as maintaining a satisfactory level of financial stability while doing work you enjoy and also finding happiness and fulfillment in your life and career choices. Career achievement is harmed if you enjoy your work but feel that it does not contribute to financial independence, and it is harmed if you are well compensated but lack pleasure or interest in your chosen profession. True career success necessitates a balance between the two.

6 Ways to Have a Successful Career

A great career can provide you with many benefits as well as real money-making opportunities. Working your way to the top will undoubtedly increase your quality of life, as we live in a world dominated by social status and wealth. There are a variety of reasons why someone would want to be successful.

One of the reasons is that being effective in your professional life may make you feel better about yourself in the eyes of others. It provides you with a sense of safety and achievement. Many jobless people having no good career have said that their lives have changed in every possible way. Following and finding out what tactics experts use, and modeling them according to your needs, is the best way to approach success.

The seven working strategies mentioned below will provide you with enough boosts to help you advance in your career.

1. Identify Your Goals

The first thing is to know yourself before considering a career path. The vast majority of people adopt a well-established trend throughout their lives. The unfortunate part is that they either don't like what they do or are unaware of how many other options are available.

To escape this horrible situation, you must first recognize your most reasonable desires. Then, go ahead and do an in-depth introspection in which you can consider the relationship between your inner impulses and your logical objectives. They must be identical. You would not be fully satisfied with your professional life if you do not do so. It takes time and effort to identify your goals, but it is a critical step in any successful person's journey.

2. Establish a Professional Curriculum Vitae

Your resume is essentially a statement that says, "I'm good at this, good at that, and I can help with this and that." That is why you should develop a professional and well-organized resume. Allowing experts to handle your resume is thought to be a wise decision.

3. Take complete ownership of your life.

One distinction between mediocre and good practitioners is their level of accountability. Even if you understand the definition, you cannot use it every day. You must expect the worst if anything negative occurs. Start taking full responsibility for your decisions and never blame anyone for your errors. That is the very worst thing a person can do. Be cool, and don't take it personally.

4. Maintain a high standard of excellence.

Another important aspect that distinguishes the good from the unsuccessful is this. Your values have an impact on how you think, believe, and act. You'll never be happy with less than you can achieve if your expectations are high. The majority of the time, people with high expectations are more competitive than the average. Take a moment every two to three months to focus on your standards and beliefs. Try to develop them little by little before you know you've reached your full potential.

5. Create a personal brand

Nowadays, branding is extremely necessary. A great amount of money is being spent by large corporations to position themselves as the "big dogs" in the marketplace. It's a tried-and-true business practice that almost every specialist firm employs. Your branding is how people perceive you in the marketplace. Professional workers should actively strengthen and market their names and services. You can easily do this by initiating a blog, building a professional social media profile, or simply offering outstanding services.

6. A lot of networking

It's all about opportunities and partnerships when it comes to networking. When you meet new people, you have the opportunity to take advantage of their abilities. You must, of course, return something: your services, your expertise, or your money. Successful people are still networking and building profitable long-term partnerships.

Create social media profiles on common platforms such as LinkedIn, Twitter, and Facebook to get started. When it comes to this form of operation, these three networks are the best options. Along the way, you'll come across several opportunities and career options. LinkedIn, for example, is brimming with industry professionals who are simultaneously branding their businesses and networking. Twitter and Facebook are often used in these situations. Facebook is useful for a variety of purposes, including networking.

Your Plan to Success

A person's strategy to evaluate career goals and the path to achieving those goals is referred to as career planning. The procedure incorporates several activities, including self-improvement measures and the method of achieving these objectives. It seems impossible to overstate the value of career preparation. Any person who wants to be successful in life needs to have a career plan. To get the desired benefits, it is a multi-stage process that must be carefully prepared and performed. But, before we get into the importance of career preparation, let's look at the different aspects of it.

Characteristics of Career Planning

Career planning is important because it allows us to map out a detailed roadmap for our professional future.

Let's overview some of the major advantages of career planning:

It will assist you in making a career decision:
Career preparation entails determining your strengths and researching areas in which you can succeed. If you've identified your strengths, you can start looking for opportunities in your chosen area. If you are good with technology, a career in digital services such as software development, AI, data science, education, data analytics, or digital marketing, for example, can be a great option.

Job security can be ensured by career planning:
Everyone wanted to be a barrister in the early twentieth century because it meant commanding respect and making a lot of money. An MBA degree was the most sought-after a few decades ago because it made breaking into the big leagues of the business world a piece of cake. Many MBA graduates are still working as entry-level employees or in jobs that do not pay well enough. For lawyers and engineers, the situation is identical. Only graduates from top

universities in these fields have a chance to succeed, at least at first. In this case, one does not opt to obtain an engineering or MBA degree merely because others do so. You will find yourself in trouble if you do this without adequately preparing for your future. One of the advantages of career preparation is that it helps you make informed decisions and enter a profession with plenty of job opportunities.

It will assist you in achieving mental tranquility:

One of the less well-known advantages of career planning is that it brings peace of mind, especially in stressful circumstances. Unemployment brings with it a lot of tension, confusion, and low self-esteem. However, if you plan your career wisely, you will be keeping an eye on work patterns, reducing the chances of financial difficulties or a lack of opportunities. One of the most important advantages of career planning is that it allows you to keep up with changing work patterns, new technology, and business demands.

CHAPTER 3
THIRTEEN FIELDS TO EXPLORE FOR YOUR CAREER

In this chapter, you will learn about the 13 major fields that might interest you and the type of job roles and opportunities they offer.

What are career fields?

Career fields are a technique of grouping together different sorts of occupations based on their commonalities. These categories assist people in narrowing down their job options to select the right path for them. People can organize different sorts of labor into career sectors to make it easier to understand. Each occupation comes with its own set of needs and responsibilities. When looking for a new job, think about what kind of professional path you want to take.

13 different fields

The following are some common career fields and employment examples in each category:

1. Engineering and architecture

People who work in architecture and planning professions are in charge of developing new structures or developing aesthetically beautiful, functional, and structurally sound surroundings. Many jobs necessitate a bachelor's or master's degree. Over the next ten years, employment in architectural and engineering occupations is expected to expand at a rate of 3%, which is about average for all occupations. A total of 74,800 new jobs are expected to be created. Engineer jobs will account for most of the predicted job growth in this group since their services will be in high demand in infrastructure rebuilding, renewable energy, oil and gas extraction, and robots. Architecture and engineering vocations pay an average of $81,440 per year. The average annual wage for all job roles in this category is higher than the national median annual wage of $39,810.

Among the jobs available in this field are:
- Aerospace Engineering and Operations Technicians
- Aerospace Engineers
- Agricultural Engineers
- Architects
- Architectural and Engineering Managers
- Biomedical Engineers
- Cartographers and Photogrammetrists
- Chemical Engineers
- Civil Engineering Technicians
- Civil Engineers
- Computer Hardware Engineers
- Construction Managers
- Drafters

- Electrical and Electronics Engineering Technicians
- Electrical and Electronics Engineers
- Electro-mechanical Technicians
- Environmental Engineering Technicians
- Environmental Engineers
- Health and Safety Engineers
- Industrial Engineering Technicians
- Industrial Engineers
- Landscape Architects
- Marine Engineers and Naval Architects
- Materials Engineers
- Mechanical Engineering Technicians
- Mechanical Engineers
- Mining and Geological Engineers
- Nuclear Engineers
- Petroleum Engineers
- Sales Engineers
- Surveying and Mapping Technicians
- Surveyors

2. Arts, Culture and Entertainment

This branch of work is dedicated to enriching people's lives via culture, art, and self-expression. These disciplines have established educational programs, but they also contain self-taught individuals with an innate skill. Students who complete the Employment in Arts, Culture, and Entertainment degree will be able to channel their creativity into successful careers in these interdisciplinary and rapidly changing industries. Students are being prepared for a variety of careers in the arts, including artistic practice, arts management, cultural institutions, museums, and commercial and creative jobs in the entertainment industry. In order to thrive, many creative enterprises rely on artists, craftspeople, musicians, and other creative employees. Whether you're searching for some work as an illustrator or a dancer, there's a career out there that will allow you to express yourself creatively while simultaneously paying the bills. This list might help you begin to consider which job path is best for you.

These are some of the jobs available in this field:
- Graphic Designer
- Cartoonist
- Interior Designer
- Craft Artist
- Architect Building Designer
- Curator
- Art Director
- Animator
- Floral Designer
- Showroom Manager
- Fashion Designer
- Toy Designer
- Tattoo Artist
- Photographer
- Colorist
- Event Planner
- Billboard Designer
- Background Singer
- Dubbing Mixer
- Band Manager
- Music Teacher
- Instrumentalist

- Dance Instructor
- Filmmaker
- Choreographer
- Fashion Editor
- Textile Designer
- Cinematographer
- Director
- Hair Stylist
- Make-up Artist

3. Business Management and Administration

For business-minded people who enjoy communicating, the fields of business, management, and administration are ideal. They work to carry out numerous processes that are required for the smooth operation of enterprises. It usually entails working in a corporate setting. Business management and administration careers provide some of the most diverse job prospects. Jobs in business management and administration direct the operations, functions, and finances of a company. The majority of jobs in this group entail reviewing, controlling, and directing operations to improve efficiency and deliver more productive results.

The following are some of the positions available in this field:
- Chief executive officer
- Entrepreneur
- Controller
- Adjuster
- Real estate agent
- Budget, cost, or systems analyst

- Operations Research Analysts
- Accountants
- Marketing manager
- Human resources manager
- Training and development specialist
- Executive assistant
- Wholesale or retail buyer
- Retail salesperson
- Meeting and convention planner
- Bookkeeper
- Financial Managers
- Business development manager
- Chief Sustainability Officers
- Regulatory Affairs Managers
- Computer Operators
- Medical Secretaries
- Data Entry Keyers
- File Clerks
- Office manager
- Secretary
- Receptionist
- Purchasing Managers
- Telephone Operators
- Stock Clerks and Order Fillers

4. Communications

The objective of reaching the right audience with the right message has never been more accessible in a society interconnected by every possible kind of communication. New types of media, backed by a ubiquitous wireless infrastructure and low-cost gear, have forever altered the way the world communicates. Previous generations bore the responsibility of creating this foundation; today's job is to construct a communication structure tailored to each application carefully. Mastering the skill of conveying a focused message to varied groups of people is the goal of the communications job field. Students who study communications learn to evaluate the requirements and preferences of readers, viewers, and listeners. They have the imagination to come up with novel ways to communicate their messages. Communications majors learn how to plan, manage, and execute initiatives, programs, and events. They must be meticulous in their attention to detail while still comprehending the broad picture. Because communications efforts are frequently criticized and fail, communications majors learn to accept negative feedback and deal with less-than-successful efforts. Communication students learn how to express a variety of concepts in a variety of situations. Public speaking, small group communication, organizational communication, and cross-cultural communication are all essential courses in most communication degrees. Learners improve their listening skills and learn to explain concepts interestingly and straightforwardly during these sessions.

These are some of the jobs available in this field:
- Public Relations Specialists
- Meeting/Event Planner
- Journalist
- College Alumni and Development Officers
- Media Planner
- Social Media Manager

- Human Resources Specialist
- Copywriter
- Communications manager
- Communications Editors
- Communications Specialist
- Marketing Communications Specialist
- Investor Relations Managers
- Public Relations Account Coordinators
- Communications Director
- Market Researchers
- Marketing Directors
- Business Reporter
- Health Educator
- Brand Manager
- Sales Representative
- Creative Supervisors
- Newscasters
- Proofreaders

5. Community and Social Services

The social and community services Jobs that provide practical support to people and communities to enrich people's lives are included in this sector. This career path is for persons who wish to enhance social institutions and services based on social justice and equality ideas. Individuals often enter this sector because they want to advocate for or support a specific group of people.

Most persons who work in social services find personal fulfillment in assisting others throughout their day. Compassion and dedication are required in most social service occupations. Workers in social services play a vital part in people's lives. Individuals who appreciate assisting others and desire to help people improve their lives are drawn to employment in social services. People who work in social services typically assist others in functioning as best they can in their surroundings. A bachelor's degree is required as a must for many social services jobs, and a graduate degree may be required for some. Some degree programs combine classroom learning with on-the-job training. Some social service jobs necessitate licensure, certification, or registration. The requirements differ depending on the field of social work and the state.

These are some of the jobs available in this field:
- Emergency Management Directors
- Rehabilitation Counselors
- Recreational Therapists
- Clergy
- Directors of Religious Activities and Education
- Religious Workers (all other)
- School counselor
- Probation Officers and Correctional Treatment Specialists
- Health Educators and Community Health Workers
- Speech pathologist
- Marriage and Family Therapists
- Rehabilitation counselor
- Social and Human Service Assistants
- Licensed clinical social worker
- Social and Community Service Managers
- Child welfare social worker
- Social Workers
- Palliative and hospice care worker

- Substance Abuse, Behavioral Disorder, and Mental Health Counselors

6. Education

The art of skillfully transmitting knowledge and information to individuals is the focus of education. Teachers are the most prominent position in this profession, although it is not restricted to them. Management, administrative, and board member positions are also available. Education careers can be one of the most satisfying ways to make a difference in people's lives. A bachelor's degree in education is a necessary initial step in becoming a teacher. Even if you don't want to teach in a traditional classroom environment, an education degree can serve as a stepping stone to a range of educational jobs, such as education administration, school counselling, or even social work. Job education assists students in developing the skills necessary to assess various career options. Students engage in hands-on instruction to master a craft, such as plumbing, automotive technology, cosmetology, or welding. In contrast to vocational training, which requires students to participate in a variety of academically oriented courses, career education requires students to participate in a variety of academically oriented courses.

These are some of the jobs available in this field:
- Special education teacher
- Community education officer
- Play therapist

- Education administrator
- Primary school teacher
- Secondary school teacher
- School principal
- Early years teacher
- Museum education officer
- Private tutor
- Superintendent
- Careers adviser
- Youth worker
- Education consultant
- Health play specialist
- Teaching assistant
- College professor
- School librarian
- Substitute teacher
- School Librarian
- Vice Principal
- School Secretary
- Special Education Teacher
- Family support worker
- Child psychotherapist
- Counsellor

7. Science and Technology

Medicine, computing, military defense, and textiles, to name a few, are all areas where science impacts our lives. New employment options emerge as new domains of research and technology emerge. For people with vocational/technical training, college diplomas, and graduate degrees, the physical, biological, earth, applied, and engineering sciences present stimulating and enriching options.

Science and technology is a broad topic that encompasses scientific research and the development of novel technologies that help humanity.

Science and technology have played a significant part in improving people's lives around the world, but all countries must reap the greatest advantage. With the advancement of medicines and disease analyses, science and technology has made life a lot easier and better. Apart from medicine, considerable progress has been made in education, communication, agriculture, industry, and other fields; worldwide economic production has expanded 17-fold in the twentieth century. Despite progress in practically every field, the world is still plagued by hunger, sickness, pollution, illiteracy, and poverty. A significant difference could be made with the correct uses of research, development, and science and technology implications in the twenty-first century. The qualification required for this field includes M.Phil. or PhD in specified subject.

This career field encompasses the following occupations:
- Archeologist
- Biologist
- Software engineer
- Chemist
- Laboratory technician
- Scientific Writer
- Researcher
- Technical writer
- Professor

- Computer Research Scientist
- Microbiologist
- Physicist
- Artificial Intelligence and Machine Learning
- Data Scientist
- Business Analyst
- Block chain Developer
- Computer Systems Analyst
- Software Designer
- Software Developer
- Web Developer
- Network and Systems Administrator
- Sales Engineer
- Space technologist
- Information Security Analyst
- Information Technology Manager
- Geologist
- Forensic pathologist
- Astrophysicist
- Computer Support Specialists

8. Installation, Repair, and Maintenance

Because most mechanical or electrical products require installation, maintenance, or repair, qualified installation, maintenance, and repair personnel have plenty of career prospects. Maintenance specialists are crucial in the repair and maintenance of equipment, machineries, and structures. Their field of study and employer determines their working environment. Machinery maintenance workers, industrial machinery mechanics, and electro-mechanical technicians are all terms used to describe maintenance technicians. There are a variety of installation, maintenance, and repair jobs available. These jobs can be found in a variety of locations. On-the-job training is required for some installation, maintenance, and repair jobs, while others require completion of a formal training program.

Preventive maintenance techniques for machinery, tools, and equipment are covered under the maintenance, installation, and repair pathway. Troubleshooting and repairing digital, electrical, electronic, and mechanical systems are all part of this job. Employees who work in the installation, repair, and maintenance field assist customers in operating specialized machinery. Workers in this industry have a broad understanding of their profession. They assist with installing, maintaining, troubleshooting, and repairing a wide range of modern products.

Among the jobs available in this field are:
- Auto mechanic
- Plumber
- Landscaper and groundskeeper
- Aircraft and Avionics Equipment Mechanics and Technicians
- Diesel Service Technicians and Mechanics
- General Maintenance and Repair Workers
- Heavy Vehicle and Mobile Equipment Service Technicians
- Medical Equipment Repairers
- Small Engine Mechanics
- Telecommunications Equipment Installers and Repairers
- Bicycle Repairers repair and service bicycles.
- Coin, Vending, and Amusement Machine Repairers
- Commercial Divers
- Camera and Photographic Equipment Repairers

- Electronic Home Entertainment Equipment Installers and Repairers
- Wind Turbine Technicians
- Home Appliance Repairers
- Recreational Vehicle Service Technicians
- Automotive Body and Glass Repairers
- Industrial Machinery Mechanics and Maintenance Workers and Millwrights
- Line Installers and Repairers
- Bicycle repairer
- Electrical and Electronics Installers and Repairers
- Heating, Air Conditioning, and Refrigeration Mechanics
- Wind turbine technician
- Tire Repairers and Changers
- Security and Fire Alarm Systems Installers
- Signal and Track Switch Repairers
- Automotive Service Technicians and Mechanics
- Watch Repairers

9. Farming, Fishing, and Forestry

Crop and animal production are two significant subsectors of agriculture, forestry, and fisheries, with three smaller subsectors of forestry and logging, fishing, and agricultural support activities. Animal production covers farms and ranches that produce animals for sale or for animal products, whereas crop production comprises farms that primarily grow crops for food and fiber. Fishermen who collect fish and shellfish to sell make up the fishing subsector, while forestry and logging businesses develop, harvest, and sell timber make up the forestry and logging subsector. The agricultural support activities subsector includes businesses that undertake various agriculture-related tasks for a fee or on a contract basis, such as soil preparation, planting, harvesting, or management. Farms, ranches, dairies, greenhouses, nurseries, orchards, and hatcheries are examples of agricultural, forestry, and fishery establishments. The operators, or those who run these agricultural firms, often own or lease the land used for production. However, like in logging, cattle grazing, and fishing, production can also occur in the country's natural environments and government-owned lands and waterways.

People who appreciate the outdoors should choose careers in farming, fishing, or forestry. This professional field is vital to society since it provides food for people. These occupations engage with ecosystems on a daily basis and manage them in a variety of ways. People may get up close and personal with wildlife and the environment. Growing and collecting plants and animals for human food is included.

Among the jobs available in this field are:
- Agricultural Equipment Operators
- Agricultural Inspectors
- Animal Breeders
- Farmworkers and Laborers
- Fishers and Related Fishing Workers
- Hunters and Trappers
- Agricultural Engineer
- Agricultural worker
- Agricultural Food Scientist
- Animal breeder

- Fallers
- Arborist
- Beekeeper
- Botanist
- Forest Health Specialist
- Forest Firefighter
- Horticulturist
- Horticulture Technician
- Landscaper
- Agronomist
- Plant Ecologist
- Nursery worker
- Forest and conservation worker
- Log Graders and Scalers
- Logging Equipment Operators
- Logging Workers
- Farm Labor Contractors
- Farmers, Ranchers, and Other Agricultural Managers
- Forest and Conservation Technicians
- Wildlife Officer

10. Government

Jobs in the government field involve working directly with government organizations on a federal, state, or municipal level. It is a broad career field that encompasses a wide range of jobs. People who want to develop in this field might get a degree in political science. To provide public services, care for veterans, carry mail, and keep the government running, the government employs millions of people. Employees in the public sector have defined wage structures, excellent benefits packages, and prospects for promotion. Many government employers provide similar career pathways to those in the private sector but with higher benefits. Government accountants and auditors, for example, often get greater vacation time and are eligible for pensions than their private-sector counterparts. Private enterprises, on the other hand, are generally able to pay larger compensation. Law enforcement, civil engineering, education, and healthcare are all in high demand in the government sector.

The following are examples of government jobs:
- School cafeteria worker
- Congressional staff
- Economist
- Administrator
- National park ranger
- Mail carrier
- Treasurer
- Firefighter
- Database administrator
- Records clerk
- Social services assistant
- Purchasing manager
- Civil engineer
- FBI special agent
- Aeronautical engineer
- Athletic Director
- Correctional Officer
- EMT
- Land surveyor
- Police officer
- Elementary school teacher

11. Health and Medicine

This occupation entails providing healthcare services to individuals. They are a necessary component of our civilization. This career frequently necessitates specific education and certification. Administration and managerial positions are available in the healthcare sector, just as they are in other businesses. Experience and expertise in medical services can be beneficial, particularly in senior positions and those in the front lines of service delivery. To break into or advance in the management field, you can earn a master's degree in health administration online. Online degrees allow you to continue working in the health field full-time or part-time while studying.

A career in medicine is one of the oldest and most respected professions; it allows you to have a truly unique impact on people's lives while also providing unparalleled job satisfaction. Medicine is truly a service, not just a profession, in which one must put others first. The arduous work and countless hours required to study medicine may appear to be a daunting task, but the ability to save lives is well worth the effort.

Here are some examples of health and medical professions:
- Anesthesiologist
- Ophthalmologist
- Epidemiologist
- Audiologist
- International aid/development worker
- Psychiatrist
- Podiatrist
- Acupuncturist

- Surgeon
- Research scientist (life sciences)
- Medical science liaison
- Clinical radiologist
- General practice doctor
- Hospital doctor
- Pathologist
- Higher education lecturer
- Medical sales representative
- Physician associate
- Naturopath
- Dental assistant
- Neurologist
- Adult nurse
- Children's nurse
- Clinical scientist, genomics
- Research scientist (life sciences)
- Veterinarian
- Physical therapist
- Medical Records Administrator
- Program Manager
- Speech Pathologist

12. Law and Public Policy

Empirical research and data play a big role in public policy careers. As a result, degree programs in public policy develop abilities in data analysis, critical thinking, and decision-making. Working with lawmakers, developing and advising government initiatives, or serving as an expert in a specialized sector are all ways to influence the course of national policy. This field of work encompasses all occupations. You can work for the government, a nonprofit organization, a think tank, or a huge for-profit corporation. Research findings are frequently used to inform laws and regulations in public policy careers. To give oral and written findings to policymakers, professionals in this discipline examine current research and speak with specialists. Policy research is carried out by the government and commercial businesses, nonprofit organizations, and think tanks. Think tanks, also known as policy institutes or research institutes, are nonprofit organizations that conduct research and advocate for specific causes. Many think tanks are also nonprofit organizations, while governments or advocacy organizations support others.

Every civilized society has a legal system to protect people's rights, interests, lives, and property. To administer the system effectively, people who can comprehend, interpret, and explain the laws to the general public are required.

Here are some examples of occupations in this field:
- Lobbyist
- Public administrator
- Paralegal
- Lawyer
- Attorney
- Corporate attorney
- Associate attorney
- Litigation attorney
- Campaign Worker
- Policy Analyst
- Congressional Aide

- Paralegal
- Politician
- Contracts lawyer
- Immigration lawyer
- Family lawyer
- Employment lawyer
- Personal injury lawyer
- Bankruptcy paralegal
- Litigation paralegal
- Trademark paralegal
- Associate general counsel
- General practice lawyer
- Corporate lawyer
- Intellectual property lawyer
- Labor relations specialist

13. Sales

Working in sales as a career path entails selling goods and services to individuals and businesses. People need to know everything there is to know about the product they are selling. Customer service is a big part of this job, so having good interpersonal skills is a big plus. Sales are both a rewarding and challenging profession. Developing the best solution for your customer and then providing them with the tools and motivation to buy from you requires detective skills, teamwork, and an understanding of human nature, as well as grit and determination. Sales is a job where you get paid based on how well you perform. The more you sell, the greater the bonus you will receive. This is an essential motivator and something that will drive a successful career for years for anyone with a competitive streak or a desire to be rewarded for their hard work. Despite the impression given by films like "Wolf of Wall Street" and TV shows like "The Apprentice," it is not a combat sport. Great salespeople collaborate with their clients rather than compete with them. Consider it a team sport in which you compete with your customers rather than against them. Your colleagues and customers will respect you for your industry knowledge, but you must work hard to earn and maintain it.

Jobs in this career field include:

- Sales associate
- Sales engineer
- Sales and Marketing Specialist
- Sales & Marketing Executive
- Sales development rep
- Account executive
- Account manager
- Customer success manager (CSM)
- Regional sales manager
- Sales operations manager
- Director of sales
- Territory Sales Officer
- Sales development representative (SDR)
- Inside sales representative
- Outside sales representative
- VP of sales
- Chief sales officer (CSO)

CHAPTER 4
SEARCHING, INTERVIEWING AND GETTING HIRED

This chapter provides you with complete knowledge regarding the job-hunting process and the difficulties people face while finding their desired jobs, and the strategies they can adapt to overcome these barriers.

Best ways for people to apply for jobs in 2021

The incidents of 2020 have had a major impact on all of our lives. The working schedules and lives of many people have been turned upside down or dramatically altered. On top of downturns in many sectors, working parents have had to combine childcare and remote education. These difficulties have resulted in a significant drop in parents of children under 18 who work. Compared to 2019, the percentage of working fathers has decreased by 5.6 percent, and the percentage of working mothers has decreased by 4.9 percent. Newly remote jobs have also experienced difficult shifts in their work lives. Most have longer workdays, putting in about an hour more every day on average and dealing with a 13% rise in meetings.

The upheavals of 2020 provided an unparalleled need for small business owners to change or fold. 92 percent of small business owners said they had to "reinvent" their business models to survive pandemic setbacks. Unfortunately, several people were unable to withstand the storm. In reality, Covid-19 forced the closure of nearly 100,000 small businesses. These significant shifts will leave any job seeker with serious concerns about how their search and potential career opportunities will pan out in the coming year.

1. Look for job openings on the internet

If you're like many job seekers today, you might believe that the easiest way to find a new job is to use the internet. Today, many work seekers spend hours browsing the most common online job boards and distributing their resumes to as many places as possible.

However, you might be amazed to learn that this isn't the most successful way to find a new career. What is the reason for this? Just about 4% of job seekers, according to some figures, find work solely via the internet. If you go with this path, make sure to supplement your online work quest with some of the other options on this list. However, work boards are useful for the following reasons:

- Research what companies are posting new work openings.
- Assess what qualities employers are looking for in people in your industry.

- Find out what experience hiring managers are looking for in applicants with your job title.
- To remain a competitive applicant, identify any holes in your credentials or education.

Look into the market for people who have your skillset.

2. Make use of LinkedIn for networking.

It is said to be the most effective platform to network and find jobs in today's market. Until 2020, over 90% of hiring managers and recruiters used LinkedIn to find and vet candidates; now, LinkedIn is the largest gathering of people discussing positions and prospects in the middle of a pandemic. Here are some simple networking tips for LinkedIn:

- Maintain a professional appearance.
- Have a large number of links (at least 250)
- Request advise from people who are familiar with you.
- Make sure your LinkedIn profile summary is strong.
- Maintain an active presence on LinkedIn. Keep your job experience and expertise current in your profile. Contact coworkers and acquaintances to see whether they can refer you to some open roles. Always remember that the grass is greener where it is watered.

3. Make direct contact with hiring managers

For two reasons, explicitly contacting a hiring manager at an organization where you want to work is a smart strategy:

- Companies usually spend hefty money on recruitment fees that could be avoided if you were hired directly. This can give you an edge and benefit over other candidates.
- It demonstrates to the hiring manager that you genuinely want to work for the company, which is always a bonus.

4. Respond to advertisements

You already know that classified ads are a great way to learn about job openings in your region or around the world. Employers can post job openings on the internet, in-store windows, or in print publications.

The good news is that this is a good way to find low- to moderate-wage jobs. In reality, nearly a quarter of those who use this approach to look for lower-paying jobs are successful. If you're looking for a higher-paying job, though, this isn't the best choice.

The same strategy is being used on local work boards and forums like Craigslist and Next-door in 2021. Look for virtual "help needed" signs on job search sites in your city.

5. Seek assistance from government departments.

When looking for work, another choice is to go to a government job placement office. There are government job offices that will help you find work. Many have career-finding training services, and the workers will also provide you with hot leads on job openings. If you're having trouble finding the leads you need, this is a choice worth considering.

6. Seek referrals.

You should have something like a network in place by now. You can create job leads by tapping into your network of colleagues, family members, former coworkers, educators, and LinkedIn contacts. Approximately one-third of severe referrals, according to some reports, can result in job placement. All you have to do is stay in touch with your contacts and inquire about future job openings.

7. Apply to your desired company

You should spend a considerable deal of time looking for businesses that match your line of work and apply by email or through their "carriers" area. This covers firms that hire but also firms that do not hire. Your chances of hearing from an enterprise that does not seem to be employing are reduced, but if they respond and show interest in your past, you will virtually have no competition at all. Aim for a mix. You want to make your majority of job searches to hiring companies (perhaps 60 or 70%). Still, it is certainly worth a shot applying to positions that do not seem to be hiring or companies that currently don't have a role that is a good match with your background listed on their website. This could certainly prove to be successful for you because a company may well have been planning to post a relevant job soon. You would be shocked at how much luck goes into a job search.

8. Register with an agency

Yes, agencies are still a pretty good shout in 2021. Even though many people have had many bad experiences with Agencies, I wouldn't rule them out, just yet anyway. Simple use the Google "near me" feature and search for agencies in your field. There are plenty in your area that I guarantee you haven't even heard about!

There are two types of recruiters that you can come across:

1) The "generalist" recruitment agency - these are those who recruit for lots of different roles and fields, and these are usually the ones with the worst reputation. However, they may benefit you, as they usually only work in specific regions, they may be able to find you work that is more local to you, which in turn can work more in your favour.

2) The "specialist" recruitment agency - as the name suggests, these agencies focus strictly on a specific niche and stick to that. These are the agencies that I personally recommend, as they have more insight and knowledge about your field, they have your best interests at

heart. They are more likely to find you a role that suits you better as they know the industry inside out.

Be sure to implement what is to come of the resume "brush up", as many recruitment agencies are flooded with applications, so you want to stand out!

When you email these companies, make sure you explain to them why you think you are a good match for the company and what you can bring them. Simply saying "I need a job" won't cut the mustard, unfortunately. Show them that you have done some research on them. It shows them that you genuinely care. Employers value that.

9. Send a video application.

Ever since the COVID-19 pandemic, most companies and recruiters have gone remote. The traditional process where you come into the office for rounds of interviews are gone (for the most part). This is one of the tactics that you can comfortably assume that the minority are not utilizing! One way in which you will certainly stand out amongst a group of candidates is by going that extra mile; yes, as an addition to your application to that role, send them a short 1-2-minute video explaining why you are suitable for the role and what you can offer. There are a couple of reasons why an organization may appreciate this form of application. Let me explain:

- A recruiter can see right through you in a video application. There is no opportunity for "faking" anything. Recruiters can see your enthusiasm, comfortability with technology, confidence, communication skills, and precision through videos, which might give them a better idea of a good fit for the role than a CV application.

- As I have already mentioned, companies are swamped with CV applications, but doing it this way is easier for the company. As the video files are easier to store and organize, they are also quicker to consume for the recruiters. Not forgetting to mention, employers are a lot more likely to view your video application instead of a CV. They would much rather have that "Real" human interaction instead of reading a boring resume.

Most common Interview Questions and how to answer them

If you're a current student searching for part-time work or a recent graduate looking for full-time work, you'll almost certainly be invited to a job interview at some point. This is excellent news. However, whether it's your first job interview after graduation or your first with a business you respect, going to a job interview can be intimidating.

Thankfully, hiring managers aren't the most inventive when it comes to questioning, but they have many tried-and-true interview questions in their back pockets. This will make it really easy and fun for you to prepare your responses, eliminate nerves, and introduce yourself in a relaxed and successful manner.

Listed below are considered and observed to be the most asked interview questions, along with tips on how to respond.

Tell me about yourself.

Most interviewers will ask this question first, so it's tempting to jump right in and start ticking off all the attributes that make you the perfect candidate for the role. But you must resist. You'll get to those questions as soon as possible. It's all about cracking the ice in this one. Rather than talking about your technical abilities, tell the interviewer about something interesting that they would find relatable. You could talk about your interests or a recent major life event that was particularly important to you. Don't forget to do volunteer work and other events. It's advantageous if you can demonstrate how, you've turned your passions into attractive work skills. For example, your interest in oil painting might translate to a high level of attention to detail.

Maintain a level of neutrality in your shared interests. If you're applying for a position where political activism is important or planned, you should keep your involvement in things like political rallies to a minimum.

What are your greatest strengths?

This is your chance to shine and adapt your talents to the needs of the employer. Which of your technical skills are you most proud of? What are some of the things that people most compliment you on? This is the time to discuss those skills if they overlap with what you know the employer is looking for. Don't overlook the importance of soft skills. Share your knowledge if you're a good listener, a lifelong learner who's always trying new things, or a flexible person who can fill various positions. Before your interview, write down your answer to this issue. Make a list of your assets and then determine which are the most important. Make a list of your responses. Then read what you've written as if you're a hiring manager. How would you react if you would have to hear the answers you just gave? Are there any warning signs? Make the required adjustments.

What are some of your weaknesses?

Isn't this a great question? "Tell us why we shouldn't recruit you," the interviewer seems to be saying. What is your reaction? If you don't already have a master plan in place to fix any vulnerabilities, don't mention them. If you confess to being disorganized, tell the interviewer you've started using some cool new software to keep you on track. Don't be afraid to be vulnerable — knowing and accepting your shortcomings demonstrates that you value self-reflection and personal development. Can't come up with a truthful answer to this question that won't jeopardize your job prospects? Consider the most recent performance evaluation. Since no one is perfect, you were probably told to work on one or two things. Now you can own up to your flaws and discuss how you want to fix them with the interviewer.

Tell me about a major accomplishment you're proud of.

Prepare to share an important professional accomplishment, as well as the evidence to back it up. Note, just as when writing a resume, the golden rule is "show, don't say." "I single-handedly turned our sales department around" is boastful, but "Under my management, our sales team did an excellent job and increased their conversion rate by 87 percent over six months" demonstrates that your efforts were successful.

What is the reason for quitting your current position?

Make sure your answer to this question is succinct and upbeat. It is not the time to criticize your new or former boss. Instead of saying, "There wasn't enough room for advancement," you might say, "I'm looking to broaden my horizons and step into a more hands-on developmental position, where I know I'd excel." If you were fired from your previous job, things get more difficult. A neutral answer, such as "Unfortunately, the business and job were a mismatch for me, so I needed to find a new challenge," is the best option.

What brought you to [Company]?

This is where your analysis skills will shine! A savvy job seeker would have spent time on the company's website and read articles about the company and its main players before interviewing to get a sense of its brand presence and community. Make a list of keywords that you see on the company's About Us, Culture, and Jobs sites. Look for adjectives that characterize the business and the people who work there. You can use words like creative or competitive in your response if you see them:

"I've always wanted to be a part of a team that innovates in a way that keeps them competitive in this industry."

Tell me about a time when you had a disagreement with a customer or coworker. What exactly did you do?

This is your chance to depict how laid-back you are. Someone disagreed with you, but you maintained your composure and persevered. You should discuss how you persuaded someone to see your perspective, especially if the position you're applying for values that capacity. (A sales position is an excellent example.) This might, however, be the ideal opportunity to demonstrate that you can collaborate and play well with others. Discuss a time when you discovered something due to a disagreement and how it changed your viewpoint.

It's all about the plot. Choose one that depicts a dispute with a positive outcome and demonstrates the willingness to cooperate and develop.

What do you think your manager and coworkers would say about you?

For a variety of factors, honesty is the best policy. Don't just pass yourself off as super effective if you're a world-class procrastinator, for example. The major key or secret to a successful interview is highlighting your strengths while also showing your ability to learn from and improve your weaknesses.

Offer examples and be descriptive. Your coworkers may claim you're a hard worker, but without a story to back it up, you're only repeating a cliché the interviewer has most likely heard hundreds of times. Instead, share a tale about a time when you went above and beyond and received praise from your coworkers and friends. If you're facing trouble while coming up with a particular example, look back at previous performance reviews. It's completely appropriate to paraphrase a favorable review:

"My manager thanked me for my ingenuity in putting together a new content plan in my most recent performance evaluation."

Where do you see yourself in the coming five years?

Most job seekers react to this question in one of two ways: aggressively competitive ("I want your job!") or overly modest ("I just want to do the best work I can and see where my skills lead me.") Neither response is likely to help you get a job. Instead, give a broad answer. Rather than saying, "My ambition is to be in a place where I can take on new challenges," say, "My goal is to be in a position where I can take on new challenges." I want to take on more management duties, so I'm looking for ways to develop my management skills."

What makes you the best fit for the job?

Don't you despise being asked this question? It's tempting to list your sterling qualities, but your rivals are likely to have many of the same qualities so that you won't stand out. Instead of listing your skills and qualifications, restate what you know about the company's needs and the job, and then explain why you're a good match. Forbes has an example of the technique in action:

"From what I've learned about the work, it appears to be a task that needs a lot of quick movement during the day, which is exactly the type of job I enjoy. I like to keep busy and wear many hats. Is my environmental evaluation accurate?"

Dress for the role you want, smile confidently, and shake hands firmly, but don't forget to do some behind-the-scenes interview preparation. It can create the difference between leaving with a bad feeling and leaving with a job.

How to negotiate the best salary possible

Negotiating a wage can be difficult for work seekers who don't understand the compensation packages that potential employers are willing to pay. Candidates who demand wages that greatly surpass a company's budget leave no space for negotiation in these situations, potentially jeopardizing the work offer.

On the other hand, being paid what your worth is important – you don't want to be exploited. You don't want to be resentful of your manager because he or she underpays you. And, of course, you must be able to pay your bills.

The tips below will assist job seekers in securing the compensation packages they deserve. The 5 Most Effective Salary Negotiation Strategies

1. Have Patience

When you're interviewing for a job, avoid the urge to inquire about pay before the boss brings it up first. If you are being asked about your wage expectations, say that you're prepared to compromise based on the essence of the work.

2. Consider the Job Offer

When you get a work offer, carefully consider it. There are more things to consider than just the starting wage. For instance, you may want to ask about the possibility of a commission, incentives, and expected wage increases, as well as benefits, hours, and opportunities for promotion and development. Both of these variables affect your net income and spending power at the end of the year. For example, the job could pay less than you expected, but if the medical and dental benefits are generous, you may save thousands of dollars in medical bills per year.

Record this information in an organized checklist for each future role and weigh the benefits and drawbacks before making a decision.

3. Take into account a counter-offer

After receiving a work offer, one of the easiest ways to start a conversation is to request a meeting to discuss the offer.

4. Figure out how much your worth.

Take the time to look at wages for the role you're interested in. Information is a powerful tool. You'll be better prepared to get what your worth in the marketplace once you've done your homework.

There are a few useful online tools to aid you in your study. Glassdoor.com, for example, allows you to study individual businesses, see what people in particular positions have earned, and read what current and former workers have to say about the employer and their careers.

Salary.com, PayScale.com, Indeed.com, and LinkedIn.com are other websites with online salary calculators. You can also use cost-of-living and paycheck calculators to figure out what you'll spend and how much you'll get paid. Keep in view that some of these sites need registration; most are free to use, but a few require paid memberships.

5. Take Your Time

If you are offered a position, do not make a hasty decision on whether or not to accept it. You should take advantage and ask follow-up questions, no matter how insignificant they might seem to be. Requesting more time to think about the bid shows that you are careful and methodical in your dealings.

Confirming the employer's deadline for an answer, asking for more details about the pay package and employee benefits, and entering discussions about the offer and the start date for your new job are the best ways to receive and use the additional time you need to make your decision.

Elbert Holden

How to adapt to your new workplace environment

Though starting a new job is exciting, adjusting to it cannot be easy. Change can be challenging. If you approach the change with the wrong strategy, it will be more challenging. Discussed below are a few suggestions to guide you in adjusting to a new work climate.

1) Pose a question

Always ask questions. Understandably, you don't want to set the precedent of requiring additional clarification when you first start but keep in mind that you're new! There will be stuff you need to know and understand because you are learning a whole new method. Asking questions does not make you seem dumb; in reality, asking the right questions has the opposite effect. The single most critical habit for creative thinkers is asking questions. Asking questions depicts that you are committed, looking forward to the day on your own, which will impress your new boss to see you as someone who will contribute fresh ideas in the future.

2) Look for a mentor.

Always look out for somebody to guide you because having a mentor can make or break your adaptation, especially at the start. This person can be anyone, i.e., a member of your department, your boss, or even a friendly coworker. They'll answer your questions and help you adjust to the community by explaining normal processes and procedures, but they can also help you jump the line on understanding some of the more important items that aren't included in the handbook. For example, where you should hide your food, how you should interact with the rest of your team, and so on. This close connection will assist you in adapting and make you feel more a part of the business.

3) Get to Know People

Try to make new work friends in addition to your mentor; it makes a difference and helps to adapt to the new working environment. Instead of feeling alone in the office, you'll feel more connected and a part of things this way. But you don't have to go around to each office and cubicle and introduce yourself. Participating in staff events and implementing the first two tips will make a big difference.

4) Focus on This Role

Most of us play the comparison game at some stages in our lives, and it typically damages us more than it benefits us. You might be excited to start this new job or career, but the flashback and memories of how happy and satisfied you were in your previous job may prevent you from making a fast transition. Focus on identifying how you can use the skills you've already mastered and appreciated the ones you're learning. Accept change and new challenges with open arms, and you'll be successful.

5) Take care of yourself.

Allowing a change of workplace to become an excuse to neglect healthy eating or exercise is not good. Taking proper care of yourself makes you happy both mentally and physically, which will help in adjusting to a new workplace. Avoid ignoring your regular healthy habits and instead concentrate on creating new ones that take into account your new responsibilities.

How to develop a good relationship with your new colleagues

The first few months in any job are crucial, and we are under a lot of pressure to prove our worth. This could include impressing our new boss or achieving a quick result. Apart from these early victories, it's important to lay the groundwork for good working relationships with our new coworkers.

It's important to thrive if you have successful working relationships. Better working relationships lead to improved teamwork, which will make you happier, more committed, and more profitable. They are the cornerstone of our success.

Given this, and the fact that many job arrangements have rapidly switched to working from home, it's important to note that the way colleagues interact has changed as well.

Here are five main points to keep in mind to help you form positive working relationships with your new coworkers:

1. Be diligent and assist wherever possible without being questioned.

As a new member of the team, your coworkers will be eager to see if you can contribute to the overall team goals and specific tasks they are working on. That will most certainly manifest itself in the job you are assigned early on; keep in mind that new workers are usually not overworked.

Give your expertise and experience to group projects wherever possible, and find a way to assist with the work your colleagues are doing. Schedule video calls to talk about how you can help and to learn more about how your team works together. Keep in mind that you do not overburden yourself and try to take on work that you are not happy with; but, if there is an opportunity to help, avail it.

2. Spare time for everybody, not just the most important people.

There's a temptation to spend all of your time and money impressing more senior stakeholders and overlooking junior colleagues and activities you consider unimportant. Don't ignore this stuff because they are important to others. This can be difficult in a new position where you're under pressure to impress and make an impression, particularly if you're working remotely in a competitive market.

However, keep in mind that a reputation is established at all levels, not just among your boss and management team.

You'll go a long way toward building long-term working relationships if you develop yourself as a dependable, supportive, and respectful member of the team among your junior colleagues, managers, and peers.

3. Always follow up with people and complete work on time.
Nothing is more annoying than somebody who repeatedly fails to keep a promise or meets deadlines. Failure to complete work or respond to emails and requests for information and assistance is the fastest way to tarnish your credibility and jeopardize future working relationships.

If you find yourself overburdened or short of time to follow up on it, it's critical to be transparent and frank with your coworkers about it. It's preferable to give someone enough notice and be truthful than to fail to deliver without explanation.

4. Make an impression in meetings
Professional partnerships are founded on mutual respect, and there's no better way to win your colleagues' respect than by demonstrating that you're a dedicated and valued team member. And what better way to demonstrate that you are here to participate than by attending

meetings? Arrive prepared, express yourself, support others' opinions, be constructive, and participate in the proceedings.

Although this could be different when working remotely, make sure your camera is turned on and regularly interact with those presenting in team meetings. This will assist the team in putting a face to your name, which will make it easier for you to learn who everyone is on the team.

5. Maintain a good attitude
Maintaining a good attitude toward your new colleagues is an important part of developing healthy relationships. There will almost certainly be some office politics and gossip – it's a fact of life when you work in such close quarters. However, as a new member of the team, you should keep your distance from this operation.

The complexities of how a large team works together and interacts are complex, and getting too caught up in gossip or politics will only cause more harm. Don't jeopardize someone's credibility by disparaging them or joining in on a joke at their cost. You'll be the subject of speculation before you know it, and it isn't easy to repair a tarnished image.

Hard work, integrity, and a positive professional demeanor are characteristics that will help you advance in your career and make an impact in any new position. You will easily create lasting working relationships by respecting your colleagues and demonstrating your importance by offering your time, knowledge, and expertise. This will take you through your first few months on the job and your long-term future with the company.

CHAPTER 5

IF THEY CAN DO IT, WHY CAN'T YOU?

<u>Inspirational Career Switching Case studies</u>

<u>How I Moved from social media to a creative artist</u>

by

Nicole Varvitsiotes

I've had one finger on my Tweet Deck and the other on the Creative Department since the beginning of my career as a Social Media Associate. Tattoos danced in the light of oversized Mac monitors as the enigmatic group huddled in the corner. They were still doodling, making things, and painting, as if they'd been styled for a photoshoot. I was drawn in by the magnetism. I aspired to work as a copywriter.

As a result, I figured it would be a good idea to sit with the Creative Director who hires the Copywriters—you know, find some common ground to schmooze on, then go in for the kill with questions about what she thinks the ideal candidate looks like to her and how I could place myself for an inter-office move.

Elbert Holden

The meeting deviated significantly from the plan. I sat back and started listening to her rattle off imaginative commandments through pursed lips rather than leaning into a hasty transition out of the world of social monitoring and status changes.

You must have a copy portfolio school diploma.
- You must have three years of advertising agency experience.
- You must be familiar with the Adobe Creative Suite applications.
- You must own at least two pairs of Wary Parker glasses, be a band member, and wear some mint at all times.

There are no exceptions. I thought it was fantastic. None of the above apply to me. I was defeated and spent weeks lamenting my defeat, splitting my time between pity parties and studying online copy colleges. For a while, I pouted over price tags and whined to friends and family — until one of my mentors, Ellen Curtis, said something that broke up my periods of intense and meaningful brooding.

"The IRL vs. the URL."

In other words, who I was in real life will never be allowed into the Creative Department. My Jan sport was still in sight at the time, and I had no postgraduate education or relevant job experience. My only hope lay in my freshly issued diploma. But who I was about to become — online, at least — could make me a sure thing. Basically, I knew I'd have to paint myself onto the internet's canvas as the wise, playful, and sharp-witted writer I desired. The portrait could then be used to manipulate attitudes and form perceptions. I would market myself as if I were a brand and handle my online image as I saw fit, ensuring that the iron-fisted dragon lady of a Creative Director would see my worth despite her valuable checklist. For the record, digitally dressing for the role I wanted (rather than the one I had) paid off, and I was hired as a Copywriter in the Creative Department six months later. Here's how dedicating time to my personal brand aided the train's departure from the station.

How I Switched Industries from the Control Room to the Cubicle

by

Ann Hynek

We are all asked as children what we want to do as we grow up. And my answer has always been "be a journalist" for as long as I can remember. I'm not sure how this term first entered my vocabulary, but I remember thinking to myself in elementary school while watching Nightly News on NBC, "That's it." That's just what I'd like to do." In 12th standard, I was one of the few students who focused my college search on a long-term career goal. My parents regarded themselves as fortunate (especially when we realized that the best journalism school in the country was just a few states away from my hometown).

Elbert Holden

After graduating from the University of Missouri with a bachelor's degree in journalism, I moved to New York City, which is known to be the birthplace of major news networks and internationally renowned publications. The holy grail in journalism. I remained for five years, following my dream work and being fortunate enough to have amazing mentors and once-in-a-lifetime opportunities. Until something odd happened: I no longer wanted to do it. The odd hours, missing Christmases, Thanksgivings, and other important events with my family, and the meager pay—what had been a fantasy had become a reality, and it had fallen short of my hopes. Despite how alarming it was, I took to heart the old New York sentiment of "only I can make it here." I went somewhere else to make it, doing something totally different, and I couldn't be happier. Here's how I did it, as well as some things to consider if you're looking to make a move.

Doing My Homework

I decided I wanted to work in financial services marketing and communications after covering the 2008 financial crisis firsthand. I'd always be able to learn something new every day and hone my craft, but I'd also be able to spend holidays with my family, as I do with news. But I was essentially starting over in my career. Where was I supposed to start? I began by approaching friends and acquaintances who served in similar roles and asked them what they liked and disliked about their jobs (usually over lunch—my treat). No subject was off-limits—this was a big, life-altering decision, and I needed all the information. Why did they apply for this job in the first place? What did they find appealing about it? What were the most difficult obstacles they had to overcome? Was there space for them to develop where they were, and could they see themselves doing it for a long time? Why do you think that is? Of course, every role has its advantages and disadvantages, but I wanted to know if the advantages outweigh the disadvantages. I was very fortunate in that people were able to be completely honest with me. I realized I was able to make a move once I got the answers I wanted. This is a critical step in the research process. It's easy to fantasize about new and different work, but a career change is a significant time commitment (and often, money). Before you decide to relocate, make sure the grass is really greener on the other side.

Resume Revamp

My next task was to convert the skills I'd gained in one area into something that would be ideal for my new job. I honed in on a few main ties after learning more about what it took to excel in financial marketing and communications: For one thing, as a financial journalist, I had spent years studying various financial concepts and had a good understanding of them. I also had a unique viewpoint on what reporters expected from publicists, such as which pitches worked and which ones didn't. I wrote these things down as bullet points on my resume and points in my cover letter, and I asked colleagues in marketing relations to serve as sources for me in the hopes of boosting my reputation. What's more, you know what?

Elbert Holden

Employers were concerned about my career path and why I was making a transition, rather than dismissing my resume because I didn't have a typical experience. After sharing my story and verifying my credentials, I discovered that most companies were willing to get a new outlook in the workplace.

So, consider how you can bring that new insight to your new career path — no matter what you do, there always needs to be something from your previous experience that's not only transferable to your new job but also exciting to potential employers.

Why Did I Give Up My Job and Row Through Three Oceans?

By
Roz Savage

Why in the world would a woman in her mid-30s, with no prior record of adventure or insanity, quit her career, abandon her husband and house, and embark on a round-the-world rowing trip?

When I declared my plan to row across the Atlantic Ocean in 2004, I'm sure several of my peers, including my mother, wondered the same thing. I kept on rowing across the Pacific Ocean from 2008 to 2010, and the Indian Ocean hence became the first woman to do so. During my time on the water, the explanation for my decision became increasingly clear — I had been hit with a double whammy of discoveries that rendered my previous life path untenable.

First, I noticed that, though my work paid well, it did not make me happy. I sat down one day and discovered and wrote two versions of my own obituary: the one I wanted and the one I was on the verge of writing if I continued down my current course. My career was not leading me in the direction I desired. In reality, it was leading me down the wrong path toward a life of indifference and duty rather than one of freedom and fulfillment.

Second, I had an epiphany about the climate, and I felt compelled to ask people to reconsider how we handle the earth. I had previously considered "the environment" to be a charitable cause or a concern in which I could choose if I should participate or not. But then it seemed to me that it was inextricably linked to life itself — something on which our continued existence is predicated. Activism had become unavoidable. Got no choice left, so I went on and participate if I cared about my own health, happiness, and well-being, not to mention humanity's continued life.

But I was nobody at the time — just a recovering management consultant and a London city burnout. It's not a particularly convincing outlet for launching an environmental awareness programmer. So, with many years of university rowing under my belt and a desire for adventure, I took up my oars for the cause, using my ocean rowing adventures to raise awareness of my appeal.

Elbert Holden

Since then, I've rowed over 15,000 miles, logged over 5 million oar strokes, and spent approximately 520 days alone at sea in a 23-foot self-contained rowboat with nothing but a large supply of audiobooks and the occasional sighting of wildlife to hold me company. Life on the ocean is difficult, with frequent drenching's, constant pain, and never-ending threats to my physical and mental equilibrium. Brief bursts of terrifying terror punctuate long stretches of crushing boredom. However, the experience has taught me two important lessons about terror.

First, fear is not anything to be afraid of. I spent a great span of my life trying to stay safe and protected to stop being afraid. However, I became concerned about losing those things. My sense of security was somehow deeply rooted in my work, my husband, and my house, but it was a frail and fragile thing that could be taken away from me in the event of a financial crisis or divorce. My sense of security now stems from the knowledge that I can deal with almost everything life—or even an ocean—can be thrown at me, but I will be optimistic.

Finally, I've discovered that fear can be overcome by a greater fear—one that gives me the strength and confidence to keep going day after day through discomfort, anger, and waves of 20 feet. Although I am concerned about the approaching hurricane, I am much more concerned about what could happen to us collectively if I, and others like me, do not continue to do whatever we can to raise awareness.

Many people have asked why I did what I did. They even question my sanity, asking, "Are you insane?" I've never quite figured out how to say this without coming across as judgmental, but when I look at the so-called "civilized" world ashore — a world in which 1 billion people are hungry and another 1 billion are overweight, a world in which single-use objects are made of plastics, a world in which we spray herbicides, pesticides, and other poisons onto our food and then eat it — I think if that's how being normal and sane is then this world really needs to be crazy.

Barriers preventing people from changing their Career

Raise your hand if you're considering a career change during COVID-19! Or maybe you're in the middle of it, but something is keeping you from moving forward. Whatever the situation may be, know that you are not the only one. Many people who want to change jobs get trapped in the process. Discussed below are among the most common challenges faced by career changers, both before and during their transition, and how to solve each one.

1. Focus on The Weaknesses

Almost anyone I speak with who is considering a career change but is stuck is focused on all the stuff they don't know how to do or all the opportunities they lack. This is backward: no one recruits you based on your lack of knowledge or experience. The single thing that matters the most is what you already know, what you've accomplished, and what you want to learn. Focus on what you can already offer any occupation, and you'll feel far more in control of your career path.

2. Uncertainty about what you want

Do you have the feeling you can get whatever you want, except you're not sure what it is? If this sounds like you when it comes to your career change, think about it: are you still unsure about what you want? Most people, in my experience, know what they want but do not know how to get it. For example, you may know that you would like to work from home and write, but you are unsure what type of job would pay you to do so. If this describes you, stop claiming you don't know what you want and instead fix the real issue: you don't know what profession can provide you with what you want. It's also possible that you know what you want but are too scared to say it because you're afraid you won't succeed. In that situation, the problem is anxiety, not a lack of understanding.

If you're unsure what you want, use this time to try something that sounds interesting. Have fun exploring, and you'll figure out what sounds best along the way.

3. Insufficient information

In my work assisting people in changing careers, I often learn about various occupations and sometimes come across occupations I had no idea existed! The reality is that you were probably only exposed to a few potential career opportunities as a child, and you have little knowledge of a wide range of occupations. Add in the fact that technological advancements are generating a slew of new possibilities that didn't exist only a few years ago, and there's a fair chance you've never heard of at least a few that might be a good fit for you. Most career changers lack sufficient information to make an educated decision; this is why you can study and evaluate potential careers and business ideas before committing to a new career to obtain a true understanding of what they are like.

4. Financial Concerns

We all know the drill: you need at least six months' worth of savings, no debt, and a full-time or part-time job. To be precise, you should be financially secure before making a career transition. If you are, and you are still worried about finances, keep reading for more advice on dealing with your fears. Concentrate on the task at hand, and as long as you maintain your financial savvy, you'll be fine.

5. Unhealed Trauma

This, in my opinion, is the huge elephant in the room, the one thing we don't tackle when it comes to career-related issues. We can, too. If we don't deal with our history properly, it can greatly affect how we interact with others. So, how does unresolved trauma impact your decision to change careers? When embarking on any transition, even a career shift, you are almost certain to face rejection and disappointment — and this can be difficult for anyone, but if you are carrying a lot of baggage from the past, a traumatic experience can feel much worse until unhealed trauma is activated. This is why dealing with your background is so crucial. Treat your career change as part of a larger healing process, and begin working with a therapist or other healing professional as soon as possible. Your deep healing will assist you in better weathering the ups and downs of your career change and allow you to live a life beyond your wildest dreams. Your urge to change careers may be part of a larger call to finally let go of whatever has been preventing you from doing so that you can soar.

6. A lack of mentors and role models

Some of us have fortunate family members who are competent and encouraging, or we might have had a cool teacher or a boss who believed in us in the past. But sometimes it doesn't happen, or the people who cheer us on have no idea what we're talking about. In this case, you can go out and build a network. This may mean seeking a mentor or meeting people who are further along in their chosen profession and learning from them through experiences, deep discussions, and rapport. Joining a community that focuses on inspiring its members is also a good idea. Several organizations promote women in technology. For example, by joining one, attending events, and networking, you can gain access to a wealth of knowledge and tools to help you break into a new sector. And you may find a great mentor or role model in a more common context due to those experiences.

7. The paralysis of analysis

Some of us get lost in our minds, trying to sort out every single move from now until we retire. Of course, since each move is accompanied by imagined disasters, a lack of real knowledge, and sometimes fear, we never feel capable of making a decision, let alone knowing enough to act. You'll permit yourself to take one step at a time until you know it's difficult to schedule your whole career transition in your head. What is the next step you think you must take to progress? Concentrate on that. And have faith that as you take the first step, you will be able to see the next and so on until you arrive at your destination.

8. You Believe the Past Is a Prediction of the Future

Just because your previous bosses were unsupportive doesn't mean your next one will be; just because you've always been underpaid doesn't mean you'll always be underpaid. We never know what the future offers, but the good news is that you can always strive for a better result. Are there any bad bosses out there? I'm sure you've picked up on the warning signs by now! Are you underpaid? Use this as inspiration to say no to low-paying jobs and instead pursue a profession or business that pays what you deserve, learn to negotiate, upgrade your skills, and so on. Recognize what has happened in the past, learn from it, and then concentrate on what you want to do in the future. Allow the future to take a gamble!

9. Trying to fit in

"I should be more outgoing, attend more networking events; I am an introvert, and people like me don't usually..." Put a stop to it right there! There is a major difference between wanting to improve as an individual and believing that someone else is better than you. The probability is that you might already have everything you need to succeed, if not all of it: accept who you are. Love yourself, concentrate on what you like and are naturally good at, have fun learning new skills and venturing outside of your comfort zone, but don't think you have to be like anyone else to be happy with your job. When you embrace yourself as you are, you will live a fulfilled life, especially in your career. You'll be more open to new opportunities, flexible on the stuff you should be flexible with, and someone people want to be around if you start there. You will find a job that is a good match for you until you quit trying to fit in.

10. Don't Make It About You

Always remember that it's not just about you. Indeed, the more personal it becomes, the more insecure and depressed you will become. Who do you want to be of use to? What makes you happy? To inspire you, these questions don't have to have world-changing answers: You can choose a job that offers a stable and secure life for your family, or you can commit to starting a company from the ground up that provides excellent health insurance to its workers because you believe in doing so. Focus on the goals and know why you're doing it, and you'll discover you have more bravery and strength than you ever imagined.

The mindset you need to successfully change your career

It's all about your mindset. Having the right attitude will make the difference between success and failure, whether you're talking about job success, starting your own company, getting through a difficult workout, or becoming a parent.

Mindsets of fixed vs. growth

Our intellect, character, and artistic capacity are all assumed to be static in a fixed mindset. In essence, you are given a hand in life and must embrace it. Believing that your qualities are indelible instills in you the ability to prove yourself over and over. A fixed mentality may cause career stagnation.

On the other hand, a growth mentality is focused on the belief that you can cultivate your critical qualities through your efforts. It is presumptively true that everyone will adapt and evolve as a result of their experiences and practice. In a growth mindset, failure is seen as a stepping stone to progress rather than a hindrance.

Developing a growth mentality is one of the most important things you can do for yourself.

Mindset is the product of our own set of strong convictions. When our perspectives no longer enable us to accomplish our objectives, we should change them according to a growth mindset. Here are five ways to cultivate a growth mentality by taking care of your mental attitude:

1. Embrace failure.
Failure should be viewed as a positive rather than a negative when cultivating a growth mindset. All experience losses. The trick is to take what you've learned from each one and use it to better your decision-making. Exceptionally good people have a history of failing their way to success. Before having his big break, Steven Spielberg was rejected three times from film school. And Oprah Winfrey got fired from her job as a news co-anchor at a Baltimore television station before launching a popular daytime talk show. A producer allegedly told her that she was "unfit for television news." "I had no

clue or even a hint about what I was in for or that this was going to be the greatest rising time of my adult life," Oprah later said.

2. Decide to learn for the rest of your life.
People who have a growth mentality consistently seek out opportunities to learn, which leads to greater job success. All should pique your interest. According to research, while less popular people read mostly for pleasure, those at the top are voracious readers of self-help books. In fact, 85% of successful people read at least two self-help or educational books per month. According to another survey, 30 percent of executives believe that a desire to keep learning is the most important trait for an employee to succeed.

3. Seek out new experiences.
Challenges are opportunities for you to move closer to your goals and to learn. "Hardships always brace ordinary people for an exceptional destiny," writes C.S. Lewis. Don't undervalue the importance of being able to resolve challenges. Do you think you've gotten too comfortable with your present job? That may be a hint that it's time to look for new challenges. After all, magic happens when you step out of your comfort zone.

4. Push yourself to new limits

Pushing yourself against what you think you can't achieve is another way to cultivate a growth mindset. In one fascinating study, participants were asked to ride as fast as they could for 4,000 meters. Participants were given the same instructions again later, but this time they could compete against an avatar of their previous journey. What they didn't realize was that the avatar was traveling at a higher rate than before. As a result, participants rode alongside their avatars and traveled far further than they had previously. Your own goals can be exceeded if you force yourself.

5. Ask for feedback

People who want to improve themselves individually and professionally are more likely to seek out and value feedback. This is because people who are growth-oriented want to improve and challenge themselves. They aren't afraid of being judged or criticized. You'll have the ability to ask for feedback and learn from it once you realize you're in control of your growth.

CHAPTER 6

THE FUTURE OF WORK

How has COVID-19 affected employment and opportunities for work?

The COVID-19 epidemic had far-reaching effects on economic activity, jobs, and our way of functioning. All of these shocks, in turn, can have a significant impact on subjective well-being. It's critical to examine how the epidemic has impacted the global labor market and the world of work and the downstream effects on workers' well-being around the world.

The global labor market and COVID-19

Global growth is expected to have shrunk by over 5% in 2020, resulting in the worst economic catastrophe in a generation. Consumer spending began to decrease sharply at the start of the year, when the pandemic broke out, particularly in retail and recreation. By April, global visits to restaurants, cafes, shopping malls, theme parks, museums, libraries, and movie theatres had dropped by about 60%, and in many European countries, by more than 80%. Nearly 15 million airline flights had been cancelled by December, an average of 50,000 per day. While the global economy began to improve in the summer, several countries were hit by a second wave of recession in the fall and winter. It appears that a full recovery to pre-pandemic levels of stability is still a long way off.

Economic downturns of this magnitude have had a significant impact on the worldwide labor market. Moreover, 90% of the world's workforce lived in nations where firm closures for at least some economic sectors were still in place as of January 2021. Unemployment has risen in many nations affected by the COVID-19 issue, yet unemployment data alone may not convey the full degree of the labor market impact for two reasons.

1) First, many people who lost their employment due to the COVID-19 pandemic are listed as "inactive" or "out of the labor force" in official statistics because they are not actively hunting for new jobs.
2) Second, many workers have had to curtail their working hours due to the pandemic, even if they are still employed. As a result, looking at total hours worked reductions provides a fuller view of the crisis's effects on the labor market.

Differences in impact between countries

The crisis's worldwide economic implications have been unequal so far, with disproportionate repercussions in developing countries. Employees in lower-middle-income nations have seen a 43 percent reduction in working hours and labor income since March 2020, compared to workers in high-income nations. People working in the informal sector, who make up a large share of the labor force in developing nations, have been particularly vulnerable. The ensuing loss in earnings is predicted to be 86 percent in low-income countries. Workers in underdeveloped nations are less likely to work remotely, putting them at greater risk of losing their jobs and catching the disease in their regular workplaces. Many governments in underdeveloped or developing countries have also been unable to provide adequate economic help to their citizens. There are significant disparities in the magnitude of the economic downturn, even among high-income countries. While public health policies in each country have molded many of these consequences, labor market policies have also significantly impacted. To cushion the economic blow, many governments have implemented fiscal stimulus programs.

Disproportionate effects of the pandemic on young people
The COVID-19 crisis has hit young people with a slew of social and economic blows. According to the International Labor Organization (ILO), when the epidemic began, around 178 million young people — one in every four of the world's working population between the ages of 15 and 24 — worked in the hardest-hit sectors. Young women, in particular, account for almost half of all youth who work in the food and lodging industry. More than 75% of young workers are also employed informally. This ratio rises to above 90% in low-income countries. As a result, there has been a significant increase in youth unemployment and inactivity.

Gendered impacts of COVID-19

Women have been disproportionately affected by the pandemic's effects on the labor market. Four out of every ten employed women worldwide work in heavily damaged industries by COVID-19, including travel, retail, food, lodging, and services. Women are also significantly more likely to be employed in domestic labor in low- and middle-income nations, a sector where three out of four workers were at risk of losing their jobs in June 2020. Women are also overrepresented in several critical sectors, such as health and social work, putting them at greater risk of physical and mental illness. Women make up more than 80% of the health workforce in several high-income countries. As a result, early estimates of gender differences in the ability to work from home and changes in employment have produced inconsistent results.

Lessons for the "future of work."

While the crisis itself may be over soon, its impact on the global labor market is certain to last. Some workers may begin to hunt for professions that are more meaningful and have strong social support networks in the aftermath of the crisis, while others may seek to prioritize earnings and job security. The dynamics of these consequences are difficult to forecast, while previous recessions' documented shifts in the labor market, expectations may provide some insight.

The impact of rapid Technological Innovation

The majority of economists think that technical innovation is a crucial driver of economic growth and human happiness. Negative cultural attitudes toward technology and its disruptive impacts may jeopardize these gains. Economic stagnation, reduced economic dynamism, and poorer living standards may result from policy actions that reflect such sentiments (and inhibit innovation).

The Effects of Innovation

Benefits accrue as a result of technological advancement. It improves residents' overall living standards by increasing production and bringing new and better goods and services to them.

- The benefits of innovation sometimes take a long time to manifest. They frequently affect a large portion of the population. The poor and future generations, who stand to benefit the most, have little or no political clout.
- Short-term disruptions are caused by innovation. As some old company models fail and some people lose their employment, these upheavals may be upsetting.
- Entrenched interests may resist change. The people who are affected are frequently well-organized and powerful. They might try to sabotage prospects for innovation and entrepreneurship, contributing to longer-term growth and prosperity.

- Policymakers have notoriously limited time horizons for making decisions. They are also more likely to hear from communities and interests who have been hurt by new technology in disproportionate numbers. This could result in:

1) legislators resisting change
2) policy measures that hinder entrepreneurship and shield incumbents from new rivals.

Technological Progress and Potential Future Risks

Robotics, artificial intelligence, and machine learning are a few major examples of emerging technologies that are rapidly evolving. These innovations may increase the speed, quality, and cost of goods and services, but they also result in the displacement of many workers. This prospect may challenge the traditional benefits approach of attaching health care and retirement savings to employers. We must consider how to provide benefits to displaced workers in an economy that employs considerably fewer people. If automation reduces job security in the future, there must be a means to provide benefits outside of the workplace. Flexible security, sometimes known as "flexicurity," is a concept for providing health care, education, and housing help to people who are not technically employed.

Furthermore, activity accounts can be used to fund lifetime learning and worker retraining. Even if society requires fewer workers, there must be ways for people to enjoy satisfying lives regardless of how they choose to spend their time. Every day, new technologies are added to the list. People can use robots, augmented reality, algorithms, and machine-to-machine interactions to assist them with various jobs. These technologies have a wide range of applications and can alter existing enterprises and personal lives. They can make people's lives easier and their personal and professional relationships better. Technology is evolving rapidly, and this is having a significant impact on the workforce.

Impact on the workforce

Emerging technologies are rapidly gaining traction, implying that they are having a significant impact on the workforce. Many significant tech companies have grown to a large economic size without employing a huge number of people. Technology is replacing labor in several industries, with disastrous effects on middle-class jobs and incomes. It was widely assumed that technology would eliminate employment for a long time while also creating new and better ones. The evidence now shows that technology is eliminating jobs while simultaneously creating new and better ones. As technology advances, machine automation may eventually permeate the economy to the point that wages no longer provide enough discretionary income or trust in the future for the majority of consumers. A downward economic spiral will follow if this issue is not addressed. Machines would do the tasks of a big portion of the 'average' people in our population at some point in the future – it could be several years or decades from now – and these people will be unable to find new jobs. Robotics, machine learning, and artificial intelligence have been discovered to replace humans and improve operational accuracy, productivity, and efficiency.

With an estimated annual growth rate of 2.6 percent, the healthcare and social assistance sector is predicted to grow the fastest. Over the next ten years, this will result in the creation of around five million additional employments. This equates to around a third of all new employment predicted to be produced. Professional services (3.5 million), construction (1.6 million), leisure and hospitality (1.3 million), state and local government (929,000), finance (751,000), and education (1.5 million) are all expected to rise (675,000). Surprisingly, in light of technological advancements, the information sector is predicted to lose jobs. According to BLS forecasts, nearly 65,000 employments will be lost there over the next decade. Even though the technology is altering many firms, it is doing so by transforming operations rather than creating more jobs. Technology can increase productivity and efficiency by reducing the number of workers required to produce the same or even higher output levels. Manufacturing is another industry that is expected to lose jobs.

As technology advances, some people, perhaps even a large number of people, will be left behind. As we shall show, there has never been a better moment to be a worker with specialized talents or the appropriate education because these individuals can generate and capture value using technology. However, there has never been a worse moment to be a worker with simply "ordinary" talents and abilities because computers, robots, and other digital technologies are rapidly acquiring these qualities. To recapitulate, sophisticated societies are at a critical juncture in terms of how we think about labor, leisure, and the distribution of social benefits. Suppose these economies require fewer workers to fulfill necessary activities, and benefits are mostly provided through full-time employment. In that case, many people may have difficulty accessing health care, pensions, and the income maintenance they require to live. This is especially concerning at a time when income inequality is high and economic distributions are severely skewed.

Even if society only requires a small number of workers, there must be opportunities for people to live fulfilling lives. Before heading to have a permanent underclass of unemployed people, we must consider handling these challenges. This comprises a series of recommendations for society's future actions. Continuous learning opportunities, arts and culture opportunities, and ways to augment incomes and benefits other than full-time jobs are needed. From a societal perspective, policies that encourage volunteerism and reward people who give to worthwhile causes make sense. People will be able to adapt to the new economic reality if these efforts are taken.

How to prepare for an uncertain world of unemployment

It's only the beginning:

- Events have been cancelled.
- Travel restrictions have been imposed.
- Working hours have been curtailed.

The coronavirus produces a lot of anxiety, job shifts, and fears about the economy's long-term impact. The ripple effects are undeniably visible worldwide, providing a timely warning that disruptions occur all the time. They strike when we least expect it. Although "black swan" incidents like this are uncommon, they serve as a reminder that anything can change at any time, regardless of your role, industry, or level of seniority. Indeed, the coronavirus has accelerated previously expected trends for the future of work, such as remote working and online communication, as well as a shift in in-demand skill sets and a new degree of essential leadership capabilities. Events like these challenge us to rise to the occasion and demonstrate our resiliency, communication skills, and capacity to adapt. Those who are agile, prepared, and have a diverse portfolio of options will win. The greatest time to plant a tree is always ten years ago, but now it is a close second. So here are a few tips on how to take control of the situation and prepare for the future:

- **Be in command of your thoughts.** You might either be a victim of circumstance or a participant in resolving the issue. Complaining and fearing the consequences for your profession or business will not change anything. A worried mind can't think clearly or effectively, either. To assist or relieve anxiety, concentrate on managing what you can.

- **Make a portfolio career.** Building several opportunities to future-proof yourself is a good idea regardless of whether your employment or industry is in jeopardy. What exactly piques your interest? What have others come to you for? How else can you share your knowledge and experience without committing yourself full-time? Consider board positions, speaking engagements, and freelance options.

- **Put your efforts into developing and owning your brand.** Individuals like to buy from people they know, like, and believe in. You don't want to be connected with a specific function or profession, especially when many duties are becoming redundant and roles are no longer relevant in the fast-changing world of work. You want to be renowned for a lot more than that. In a nutshell, it's about demonstrating the value that only you can provide. Clarify your skills and what you want to be recognized for, articulate your point of difference, and disseminate your message via social media platforms such as LinkedIn. You can commercialize your opportunities as your visibility grows.

You have only two major choices when faced with a difficult scenario. The first alternative is to bury your head in the sand and become scared, resentful, and victimized. Accepting the circumstance as a challenge and taking action is the second — more positive and more effective approach. Disruptions should be viewed as opportunities to reinvent yourself and chase new chances. Now might be the best moment to start working in the profession you've always desired.

Preparing for Post COVID World

We are all facing an uncertain and unpredictable future. For many businesses, the next six months will be about surviving. Others may have the chance to concentrate on how to emerge from the crisis as a stronger, better-positioned, and more valuable company. Whatever your goal, we feel it is critical to take steps to prepare your company for the post-COVID-19 era while also caring for your employees and other stakeholders.

Capital search: Creativity needed to excel

There are no easy words to describe how difficult the coming months will be. Even robust, well-capitalized, and well-managed firms will have to work hard to manage cash and preserve company continuity. Some previously thought to be viable firms will fail because they are facing a period of no revenue. However, certain industries are struggling to meet increased demand. Those who find themselves in need of additional funds should think outside the box as much as possible. Companies suffering significant, temporary headwinds, as well as those striving to meet a sudden increase in demand, should broaden their search.

Portfolio optimization

While the economic effects of the viral infection are expected to be short-lived, the psychological effects are likely to be long-lasting. The world after COVID-19 will be considerably different. Distinguishing transient from structural changes will be key to your company's post-COVID-19 success. Large corporations should dynamically examine which assets will thrive in the new world to optimize their potential to benefit from the rebound when it arrives.

Be agile and proactive to maximize value.

The fact that asset valuations have dropped does not imply that vendors' expectations have changed. During periods of uncertainty, M&A activity tends to decline. Companies in need of finance, on the other hand, might welcome investment from new well-capitalized partners. Now is a wonderful moment for trade buyers and private equity to make a wish list of assets where a future investment or collaboration could be mutually beneficial. It could even be a chance to reintroduce previously hesitant targets. Companies that are capable and ready to act may be able to benefit from others' inaction.

Reimagine your supply chain by looking up and down.

For many businesses, the quality and viability of both their suppliers and customers will determine their ability to stay in business. For some, this will necessitate a total rethinking of their value chain. One US food company has given office workers jobs in its facilities to cope with an unexpected acceleration to double-digit growth. In China, some firms, such as HEMA – an online grocery retailer now being built by Alibaba – have responded by providing extra layers of information on their products and, more significantly, the people who transport the 'final mile.'

How to manage your finances during and post COVID-19

It's a scary and stressful moment if you've had to take time off work, have been furloughed (temporarily not working for your employer but still on their salary), or are out of work due to the coronavirus outbreak. Whatever your circumstances, you may be anxious about your funds and how you will handle them.

Familiarize yourself with your rights

Whether you're self-employed or afraid about losing your job, knowing your rights at work will help you know what you're entitled to.

Make an emergency budget.

Examine how much money you have now, what you intend to earn in the coming months, and how much you're spending. This isn't an enjoyable activity, but it's important to have a hold on what's going on, and once you've completed it, you'll likely feel more in control.

Figure out how you can cut down necessary spending

You must spend money on some items, such as electricity, rent, and food. However, there are ways to save money by reducing some of these expenses.

Utility services (water, electricity, gas)

Even though we are spending more time indoors, you may try to save money on your power and water bills by turning off lights, disconnecting things that aren't in use, taking shorter showers to use less water, and turning down the heat and layering up.

If you're having trouble paying your payments, your most recent bill will have a phone number to contact to speak with your provider. They'll be able to inform you about options for making manageable payments, as well as whether you're on the optimal tariff for the amount of electricity/water/etc. you use.

Rent/mortgage

If you're having trouble paying your rent, you should contact your landlord as quickly as possible to discuss your options. If you reach an arrangement, such as a rent decrease or late payments, be careful to obtain it in writing.

Food

Meal preparation can be really beneficial in terms of food. This entails creating a large batch of food once a week, portioning it out, and freezing it so you may enjoy breakfasts, lunches, and dinners later in the week or for several months! There are also additional strategies to reduce your food spending. If you are currently unable to purchase food, there are food banks located throughout the country to assist you.

Reduce non-essential costs

If you enjoy live sports, it's probably time to cancel your BT/Sky Sports membership and get a new one, as there are now very few sporting events going on. It could also be a helpful idea to put your beauty box subscriptions on hold for a spell. Services like Now TV and Amazon Prime frequently run promotions where you may watch some free streaming TV for a limited time (usually for a month). Simply set a reminder in your calendar to ensure that you cancel it in time to avoid being charged.

Dip into savings

You must have some money in the bank that you could use. Due to the current scenario, banks are becoming more flexible, and you may be able to access your money without incurring a fee if you have an ISA or other fixed-term or notice savings account. To see if this is an option for you, contact your bank or building society.

Access the help you're entitled to

If you cannot work or if your income has decreased due to coronavirus measures, you should apply for benefits and other financial assistance as soon as possible. If you're sick with coronavirus or have to self-isolate because of it, you can be eligible for Statutory Sick Pay (SSP). There has also been a slew of new or updated options to seek extra financial assistance to help individuals cope with the coronavirus (COVID-19) outbreak. In Scotland, for example, you can apply to the Scottish Welfare Fund for a crisis payment.

CHAPTER 7
EDUCATION, EXPERIENCE AND CREDIBILITY

How fresh graduates can find jobs in 2021

Finding a job after graduating is a significant life event. And people deal with it in a variety of ways. To avoid the change, some new graduates will take their time and travel. Others will be eager to begin their professional careers as soon as possible.

Regardless of when you intend to look for a job as a new graduate, the process can be difficult. Many graduates are unfamiliar with the fundamentals of job hunting and how to sell themselves to employers when they have little or no work experience.

Not to worry, we'll go over some of the best job-search strategies for recent graduates, including

- Setting up your job search expectations.
- The significance of a well-written resume for recent graduates
- How do you find job openings?
- Increasing your professional standing

1) How to Setup Your Expectations as a Recent Graduate

Unless you're extremely lucky, you won't be able to find your ideal job right after graduation. Sorry to burst your bubble, but it's critical to maintain realistic expectations. This isn't to say that you shouldn't try your hardest to get a great job. However, keep in mind that there are thousands of other recent graduates looking to start their careers. And there aren't many "amazing" jobs available for people with little experience. You might discover that your preferred company or ideal role has a limited number of openings. In this case, be adaptable. Look for opportunities that deviate from these ideals slightly. Keep your interests and background in mind at all times. Just don't limit yourself too much about how you can put your skills and experience to use.

2) Have your resume ready to go.

Make sure to have a resume or CV ready to send to recruiters or other contacts before you begin your job search. There aren't many employers who don't require you to submit one or the other as part of their hiring process. If you're a recent graduate seeking a professional job, your resume or CV should reflect that. To make a visual impact on recruiters, you should pay close attention to layout and design. On this front, a resume builder can assist. But it's the content you include that matters the most.

As a recent graduate, your best strategy for creating a resume/CV is to start with a template that you can tweak to fit the various positions you'll be applying for. Avoid sending the same resume/CV to every job application.

3) Identifying Opportunities: It's All About Offline

One of the most common mistakes fresh graduates make, is relying solely on online searches when looking for work. Many businesses post job openings on their websites, aggregated on sites like Indeed or LinkedIn.

However, what you find online is only a small portion of the available jobs. Many businesses prefer to hire new employees through referrals or word of mouth. Furthermore, the process of looking for and applying for jobs via online applications can be time-consuming. There is a more efficient way to do it, known as the "disruptive job search." The idea is that you research the companies or positions that interest you and then figure out how to network your way into those positions. In other words, you avoid the online application process by reaching out to employers ahead of time.

4) Establish a Professional Image

It's time to look and act professionally now that you're no longer in university and want a professional job. That means being particularly aware of the image you project, especially online. You can be sure that as your network and connect with recruiters; they will look you

The Career Change Quest

up on the internet. Take proper advantage of social media in your job search. However, be cautious about the content you make available to the public.

Do a full audit of any of your online profiles and review your privacy settings before you start circulating applications to organizations, so you know what potential employers will see if they search your name.

Make an effort not to become overwhelmed by your job search. As a recent graduate, it's easy to feel torn between all of your options. Moreover, seeing your friends find jobs may add to your stress. Remember that this is only the beginning of your career, and it's likely that you'll change jobs several times throughout your career.

Most Demanding Jobs in Next 5 Years

Indeed, has compiled a list of 15 in-demand jobs with "the most anticipated growth rates for the next five years" for people looking for a job or a new career path altogether.

The most in-demand jobs are listed below:

1. Home health aide

Home health aides assist clients with daily tasks such as dressing and personal hygiene, ensuring that clients take their medications on time, and collaborating with medical professionals to maintain a client's health. Home health aides serve many older adults.

2. Nursing assistant

Nursing assistants work in medical facilities such as hospitals and nursing homes under the supervision of registered nurses. They are responsible for taking vital signs, assisting patients with personal hygiene, serving food, and keeping track of patients' health.

3. Construction Worker

Construction workers clean up construction sites, erect scaffolding for buildings, operate machinery that transports building materials and assist any craft workers on the job. Some construction jobs may require prior training from a trade school or an apprenticeship.

4. Physical therapist's assistant

Physical therapy assistants assist physical therapists by assisting patients during appointments, setting up equipment for future appointments, and performing administrative tasks such as answering the phone.

5. Medical technologist

Medical technologists are responsible for operating medical equipment that analyses bodily fluids such as urine and blood. They maintain samples, report on the results of bodily fluids tests, and collaborate with medical experts to diagnose the results.

6.Truck driver

Truck drivers transport goods from one location to another, such as from warehouses to retail outlets. They're frequently tasked with long-distance driving and cargo loading and unloading.

7. Analyst in operations research

Analysts in operations research gather information about a company's operations. They speak with employees to identify workflow issues, devise solutions using statistical simulations, and finally advise upper management on the best course of action for the company and its output.

8. Financial advisor

Individuals need financial advisors to help them manage their personal finances. This could include making short- and long-term plans, navigating debt repayment, and assisting with investment selection. Advisors can earn money in several ways, including commissions and charging for their time.

9. Health services administrator

A health services administrator is in charge of a hospitals or other health-related organization's various operations. These tasks include ordering and keeping track of supplies, creating employee schedules, and informing employees about policy changes.

10. Registered nurse

Among other things, registered nurses administer medications and treatments to patients, teach patients and their families how to manage illnesses and injuries, perform tests and analyze results, and keep track of their medical histories and symptoms.

11. Web developer

Web developers create client websites using coding languages such as HTML and JavaScript, create website content, and maintain the websites they've created, including troubleshooting any user issues.

12. Physical therapist

Physical therapists use exercise, stretching, and various equipment to help people improve mobility and manage pain after an injury.

13. Information security analyst

Information security analysts ensure the security of computer systems by monitoring for potential breaches and implementing security infrastructure in a company.

14. Statistician

Statisticians collect and analyze data in a specific field, such as agriculture or health care. They theorize about future scenarios and solve problems in those fields using their math and statistical skills.

15. Software developer

The purpose of software development is to meet the needs of users. They create computer programs and smartphone apps, monitor the efficiency of their systems, and make any necessary updates to keep everything running smoothly.

How to brush up your CV (Resume) and Cover Letter

Having an attractive CV and a cover letter is a must to get the desired job. Follow the below-mentioned steps to improve your cv and make it stand out.

Remove any excess.

Employers would want to look at the relevant information that makes you a good candidate for an interview, so it's up to you to provide it clearly and concisely. Make sure you use plain English, avoid clichés and jargon, and don't ramble. It's tempting to cram everything you can into your resume to sell yourself, but facts, figures, and accomplishments will help you stand out. At the interview, you can dazzle them with the rest! If your CV is longer than two pages, you should consider editing it.

Elbert Holden

Clean it up.

Your CV's presentation is just as important as its content, so make sure to evenly space items and break up long paragraphs with line breaks. Instead of listing key statistics in sentences, use bullet points to draw the reader's attention to them. Fonts such as Times New Roman that are fussy should be avoided. To make it easy to read, use a simple, clean font like Arial, Verdana, or Tahoma. Try it right now and see how much of a difference it makes! Font sizes should never be reduced to less than 10 points. Bold, italics, and underlining are acceptable but don't overdo it.

Include a statement about yourself.

If you get it right, a good personal statement can be extremely effective. Keep it short and sweet, emphasizing your level of experience, strongest skills, and personal and professional qualities that qualify you for the position. If you're having trouble, have a trusted friend or colleague write down your strengths for you. It's possible that you'll be surprised and flattered!

Quantify your achievements.

It's fine to say you increased sales, but saying you increased sales by 50% to £100k per month will make any employer salivate. When mentioning revenue or cost savings, use supporting figures whenever possible. If the changes you made were related to performance or processes, make sure you explain how they benefited the company.

5 Simple Ways to Improve Your Cover Letter:

Address your cover letter to the appropriate individual: Finding the name of the appropriate person to whom you should address your cover letter will make it stand out. If the name isn't listed on the internship or job posting, try calling the company to determine who the hiring manager or department supervisor is. Avoid using the ineffective and overused "To Whom It May Concern" to get noticed.

Attract the reader's attention: Because of a weak cover letter, many cover letters and resumes are immediately discarded. Starting at the beginning is the best place to start when writing a strong cover letter. It's critical to include something in the first paragraph to pique the reader's interest. You can get the reader's attention and make them want to read more by using key terms. Make sure each cover letter is tailored to the position you're applying for, and avoid the temptation of sending the same (or very similar) letter to multiple employers.

Make your cover letter stand out: Make your cover letter stand out by including something unique. It could be a previous academic experience, internship, or job that catches the employer's attention. It could also be a specific accomplishment, such as an honor or award, that will pique the reader's interest and help you get into the current group of applicants' "yes" pile. If you've completed a study abroad programmer, this could be a great way to demonstrate your individuality as well as your ability to adapt and work with others.

Ensure your cover letter is free of errors: In a cover letter or resume, spelling and grammatical errors are not acceptable. If you send in a document that isn't error-free, no matter how qualified you are for the internship or job, your chances of being called in for an interview will be less.

Ask for an interview: Since you've followed the top four tips and The Top Steps for Improving Your Resume, now it's time to ask for an interview. Why not include your specific request right in the body of your cover letter, since the goal of writing a great resume and cover letter is to get an interview? "I am very excited about this internship or job opportunity with the (Organization name) Corporation and would be happy to answer any questions over the phone," as an example. During the winter break, I'm also available for an interview at any time.

How to get a job without experience

Finding a new job without relevant industry experience can be difficult, whether you're looking for an entry-level position right out of college or switching industries. Employers frequently prefer candidates with relevant work experience over those without, leaving you to wonder, "How do I get experience if no one will hire me?" You'll need the required educational qualifications to get a job in a new industry, but you can transfer experience from previous positions. Here are six tips to help you land the job if you don't have any industry experience.

1. Emphasize your transferable skills.
Analyze your past activities and highlight transferable experiences, which is something that every job seeker should do. This can be done regardless of your work history, but it is particularly important for those looking to change industries or start a new career. If you don't have any experience in the industry you want to work in, chances are you have some transferable work experience that fits the job description.

2. Gain experience in a variety of ways.
Do whatever it takes to improve the weakest part of your resume, even if it means picking up a part-time minimum-wage job to gain experience. Extracurricular activities, clubs, professional associations, and volunteer opportunities are good places to get more experience. Taking on a leadership role within these opportunities can be especially beneficial in demonstrating your ability to take the initiative.

3. Take advantage of opportunities for hands-on learning.
Pursuing hands-on learning opportunities is another way to gain experience. These allow you to broaden your knowledge beyond what you learned in school and provide you with real-world experience in the industry you want to break into. Even taking on a

small project can help you learn more about a field and provide you with interesting topics to talk about during an interview.

4. Begin at the bottom and work for free.
If you can't find a paid internship or apprenticeship, consider working for free to gain professional experience. If there is no open position at the company you want to work for right now, go ahead and apply anyway by offering your services for free. This can be a fantastic way to gain experience and network with professionals.

5. Network your way up the ladder.
Networking is the most important strategy that job seekers can employ. Rather than applying for any job that interests you, look for connections to teach you about a position or company. Networking is a long-term process that can occur on social media, at an in-person event, or through an online networking website. Don't ask for a job recommendation if you're a braggart; it'll turn most people off. Instead, conduct informational interviews to learn more about the company, industry, or position you're interested in and maintain ongoing relationships with industry experts.

6. Highlight your soft skills.
You can highlight many non-industry-specific skills on your application and resume when advertising yourself to an employer – these are your soft skills. Regardless of the industry, soft skills can be learned and demonstrated through any type of work experience.

These uncatchable skills, also known as leadership intangibles, are important, according to Owners, because they can help determine a potential employee's success.

7. Build your personal brand

The real problem is not the lack of experience. It's the lack of your brand and being able to sell yourself for the role. There is no doubt that a personal brand sticks you out from the crowd. Think of it like this, as an employer, what do you think they'd want from someone who was a perfect candidate for the position? The employer wants someone who can demonstrate who they are, demonstrate a positive demeanour. If you are a confident person, don't be afraid to exhibit this in the interview. Employer's value confident employees. If you want to show your eager demeanour, show that by saying, "I cannot wait to get started with this role and crush it". Above all, though, you want to demonstrate your value to the employer. How can you take a successful achievement you had in the past and project it for this role? It's not about whether the knowledge and experience that you have gained up until this point are relevant to the position you are applying for; it's about how you can relate that to this position and become an asset for that company.

What if I have no education?

Suppose you've found your dream career and you're a perfect fit for the position. In that case, you have the abilities, experience, and desire to not only fulfill the role but also to become a top performer — but if you don't meet the degree criteria, don't panic; the strategies listed below will help you acquire that job even if you're underqualified.

Highlight your relevant skills.

Even if you have a minor disadvantage regarding qualifications, you can still compete with fully qualified job seekers by emphasizing what you do have. Examining the job ad's responsibilities in detail might assist you in determining the keywords that will help your resume stand out. Use the identical terminology in your resume if a job requires a development associate with experience obtaining and cultivating significant gift donors. Also, emphasize your work experience's transferable talents.

The education portion of your CV should be beefed up.

Even if you have a bachelor's or associate's degree that has nothing to do with the job advertising, it's still worth putting on your resume under the "education and credentials" area. You can still highlight your accomplishments if you don't have a college diploma. Create a section on your resume called "honors and awards" and add any professional certificates, training programs, or other educational credentials you have. Another strategy to improve your CV is to include testimonials. Request a one- to the two-sentence endorsement of your abilities from former supervisors or coworkers (three is a good number).

Make contact with a company employee.

According to Wolfgang, obtaining a referral from a corporate employee could provide you with a foot in the door for a job interview. Begin by looking through your current network. There are alternative options for finding an advocate if you don't have a first- or second-degree relationship with the organization. "You may find out from the person how firm the degree requirements for the position are once you've discovered someone on the inside."

Prepare to discuss it at your job interview.

Although you don't want to bring up the fact that you lack the necessary educational credentials during a job interview, you should be prepared to discuss it. If the interviewer responds, "I notice you don't have a bachelor's degree in communications," the ideal response is "You're right." I don't have a communications bachelor's degree but what I do have is that qualifies me for this position."

Prepare two or three anecdotes on unique professional accomplishments that may be beneficial in this position. Explaining how you addressed a problem, went above and beyond to close a sale, or saved money on a project are all examples of this.

Finish your resume with a professional look.

If you don't have a degree, that doesn't imply you won't be a good fit for a position. It's now time to persuade a hiring manager. Knowing how to format your resume is crucial if you want to catch their attention—especially if you don't meet all of the standards.

Jobs That Do Not Require a degree

There are plenty of work alternatives for folks without a degree if you don't want to spend years in education. These jobs range from those that require only a high school diploma to those that demand some postsecondary education and training. Among them are the following:

- Licensed Practical and Licensed Vocational Nurse
- Medical Records Technician
- Bus Driver
- Patrol Officer
- Firefighter
- Insurance Sales Agent
- Recreation and Fitness Worker
- Restaurant Cook
- Plumber
- Maintenance and Repair Worker, and the list goes on.

CHAPTER 8
FOR THE ENTREPENEURIAL MINDED

Opportunities of COVID-19 Crisis

The coronavirus pandemic has several negative aspects. People get sick and die worldwide; schools close, the healthcare system is overburdened, employees lose their jobs, businesses fail, stock markets crash, and countries are forced to spend billions on bailouts and medical help. Covid-19 is a big stressor for everyone, whether directly affected or not, upsetting our psyche and prompting our anxieties. There are benefits to all of this, no matter how serious or terrible it is. By looking on the positive side, we can see a few available options throughout the COVID19 era.

Opportunity 1: More time

In today's overheated economy, time is frequently seen as the most valuable and limited resource we possess. Because we've packed our week with social meetings and amusement, such as attending the theatre, birthday parties, cinema, restaurant, bar, sports club, gym, music, festivals, concerts, and more, Covid-19 demonstrates why. Suddenly, everything is cancelled or prohibited, providing us a large amount of extra time. Even so, life continues. This demonstrates how simple it is to free our schedules. This does not apply to the healthcare industry or other critical areas, but it does apply to the vast majority of other industries. We have the opportunity to spend this time doing anything else—or, better yet, doing nothing and enjoying the free time.

Opportunity 2: Reflect and reconsider
The disruption caused by the COVID in our daily lives provides an opportunity to think and reassess what we do, how we do it, and why we do it. Things we used to take for granted, such as going to the gym, are now no longer possible. Furthermore, many people have been forced to adjust their working habits and work from home rather than in an office. Resultantly, many of our daily habits are disrupted. This is an excellent time to reconsider and adjust our habits and routines. Now that you can't go to the restaurant twice a week, commute for two hours every day, hang out with your friends, or go to a party every weekend, you can consider whether you truly want to do so after the crisis is over. The virus causes you to modify your everyday routine that you may wish to maintain even afterwards.

Opportunity 3: Speed and innovation
Slow procedures, complex bureaucracy, and strict hierarchies plague many firms, making life at the workplace less than enjoyable. Many have been compelled to break through these restrictive processes and act quickly due to the coronavirus. Procedures can be skipped or accelerated, rules can be deviated from, and choices can be taken more independently without formal approval. Employees are

suddenly allowed to work from home without being supervised. Covid-19 demonstrates that things can alter when given a powerful enough stimulus. As a result, surprising breakthroughs emerge.

Opportunity 4: Better meetings

We've had to reconsider how we handle meetings as a result of the current predicament. Many meetings are cancelled since it is no longer legal in many countries to meet with a group of large people. And when they do happen, they are usually virtual and brief. As a result, it presents a fantastic opportunity to resolve one of the most irritating aspects of organizational life. The technology for this has been available and mature for a few years, but the coronavirus has created an urgent demand for it. The real opportunity here is to implement systemic improvements that will make meetings more productive even after the crisis has passed.

Opportunity 5: Reconnect and help

Difficult circumstances provide an excellent opportunity for social bonding and other forms of interacting with and supporting others. Of course, not seeing friends or relatives has heightened feelings of isolation and loneliness in some people. However, the sense of "we're all in this together" has sparked new connecting forms. Some of these have gone viral, such as Italians singing together from their balconies and windows, but there are also numerous tiny, local initiatives to connect and assist those in need. This enables possibilities to reconnect and develop more social cohesion in the individualized societies that many of us live in. Not just amid the crisis but also later.

Opportunity 6: Cleaner environment

The virus resulted in a complete shutdown or a significant reduction in industrial activity. Factories have stopped or are operating at a fraction of their capacity, road traffic has plummeted, air travel has collapsed, and the lack of tourists has left the streets deserted. While this is poor news for most people, particularly those employed in the affected industries, it is good news for the environment. Covid-19 reduces greenhouse gas emissions and other damaging outputs in the air, water, and land.

Opportunity 7: Modesty and acceptance

The last opportunity presented by the Covid-19 crisis is an opportunity to raise awareness of our moderate influence on the earth and understand that things do not always go as we like. The Covid-19 is a global problem that has never been seen before in modern times of peace. Other pandemics, such as SARS, occurred, although their impact was less significant. We also had the 1973 oil crisis, which was a man-made disaster. Although humans did not create the coronavirus, it continues to cause havoc around the world. As a result, the virus demonstrates that no matter how well-planned and organized we are, we are powerless no matter how much we live in the Anthropocene (the epoch marked by a considerable human impact). A simple virus is throwing everything off. This is a fantastic opportunity. We want to be in charge of practically every element of our lives. Whether it's our health, airline safety, or our calendars, we have the delusion that we can have complete control over everything. The virus may be able to assist us in raising awareness that this is not the case. It allows us to play a more modest role and realize that many things are just out of our hands.

Traits that all entrepreneurs should have

Although you may never enter the ranks of multi-billionaires, these qualities of an entrepreneur can help you advance in your career.

1. Passion

Entrepreneurs aren't only looking for a quick buck. While it may be a plus, the main reward is being able to do what they enjoy. It takes a lot of time and work to start a business. It entails working longer hours and doing additional tasks. You won't want to put in the effort required to succeed if you don't enjoy what you're doing. Because they are so focused on their ambition and goal, entrepreneurs aren't frightened of spending long hours. Even in a challenging situation, they don't give up. They don't give up on their dream and see it through.

2. Motivation

Entrepreneurs are passionate about what they do. They don't rely on a boss or coworker to drive them toward their objectives or complete their tasks. Their motivation comes from within, which allows them to motivate others. Entrepreneurs understand how to express their vision and entice people to join them on their quest for success.

3. Optimism

It can feel impossible to get your business off the ground when you're just starting. Entrepreneurs, on the other hand, do not think in this manner. They have a positive outlook on the future and are continuously looking forward. You must be goal-oriented to be a successful entrepreneur. Setting goals, though, isn't enough. Make a strategy and do everything you can to achieve your objectives. There must be a reason for everything you do.

4. Creativity

Entrepreneurs think very differently than the rest of us. They have a unique perspective on the world and think outside of the box. Businesses are built on great ideas, and those great ideas must come from a place of creativity, from a different way of thinking than everyone else. Entrepreneurs are constantly seeking new ways to do things and methods to improve them. They are dissatisfied with the current situation. They come up with concepts that transform the world by being innovative.

5. Risk-Takers

When you're establishing a new firm, taking risks is unavoidable. Taking chances, on the other hand, should not be a source of anxiety for you. It's critical to attaining your objectives, and successful entrepreneurs recognize this. You'll never get anywhere if you're hesitant to take the risk. You will never be able to reach greatness if you remain complacent. Uncertainty and the possibility of failure do not deter entrepreneurs from accomplishing their goals. Entrepreneurs, on the other hand, see challenges and dangers as opportunities rather than problems.

Tests for Evaluating Entrepreneurial Potential

Many professionals who help others start businesses indicate that they have a good "feel" of whether or not they have what it takes to be a successful business owner after assisting a few people. However, you might not have a lot of self-employment examples to deal with. You'll probably feel better at ease adopting a more objective method of determining self-employment prospects to defend your judgments and activities.

There are numerous tests available in publications, on the internet, and in books that claim to evaluate whether or not a person has entrepreneurial qualities or is ready to start a firm. Unfortunately, rather than business owners, most have been developed mostly from interviews with successful entrepreneurs.

Also, only a few of these have been put to the test to see if they work. Professionals in company development and marketing warn against relying on flawed tests to decide whether or not to pursue a prospective firm. The Entrepreneur's Inventory and the Rate Your

Entrepreneurial Potential are two examples of these assessments. These tests can be used to start conversations about self-employment interest, skills, or personality traits and preparation. VR should not use them to assess support for a person's proposed enterprise. If you decide to use them, exercise caution.

Before you use one, do a personal assessment based on the following criteria:

- The questions are typically transparent or leading, allowing people who want to start a business quickly figure out the correct answers and appear to have entrepreneurial qualities.
- Many of the examinations demand binary replies, such as yes-no or true-false. This is problematic because:

1. Anyone can answer "yes" if they have done something even once. It does not assess the strength of a person's trait (e.g., a person may possess a trait but not rate it highly on a scale of 1 to 5).
2. There is no opportunity for a person to explain his or her answer.

Many of the characteristics associated with entrepreneurs may not apply to all entrepreneurs or business owners. Interviews and surveys of Caucasian males aged 30 to 40 years old were used to create the qualities indicated on these evaluations. Use caution when interpreting the findings of these tests because they are culturally and sexually biased.

Twenty (20) side hustles to start

If you're looking for a means to supplement your income with a side hustle, you're likely to come across hundreds of options. However, depending on your specific requirements and abilities, making a decent living and doing so quickly may be well within your grasp. Making money is not a constant and never-ending battle anymore, regardless of where you're from or what you do for a living, thanks to the conveniences provided by the internet. With the symbolic world at your fingertips, you may earn some extra cash even if you're in a tight spot if you know how to tap into the massive amount of opportunities present in the digital ether of cyberspace. Some of the tactics outlined below are quick ways to make money, while others require a significant amount of work. In any case, use an approach that fits your skill set and ensures that you give significant value.

1. Use eBay or Craigslist to sell your items.

Selling stuff on eBay or Craigslist is one of the safest ways to make money when you're in a pinch. Any used objects, such as furniture, household appliances, collectibles, or anything else that isn't being utilized or collecting dust, can be sold online for a profit. If you're serious about it, you could even do it for others professionally and earn a little percentage on each transaction. You'll be in terrific condition if you take decent images and write a solid description.

2. Work as an Uber or Lyft driver.

Driving for Uber or Lyft is one of the most readily available ways to earn money. Uber and Lyft are at the vanguard of the sharing economy, which has erupted. The great part is that you can use these networks to turn on and off your availability with the touch of a button, thereby allowing you to earn money at any time of day or night.

3. Deliver for Post Mates.

Another source to increase your income is to deliver for PostMates. You can work whenever you choose, just like with Uber and Lyft. While the income isn't great, you do have the opportunity to earn tips. This is a terrific method to earn money if you live in a heavily travelled region like Los Angeles or New York City, and you don't even need a car.

4. Use Airbnb to rent out your extra space.

Airbnb is a fantastic resource for folks who want to rent out a spare room or their full home. If you need some quick cash, Airbnb is a viable option. You'll get reimbursed 24 hours after a guest checks in, which helps to eliminate any potential difficulties or frauds. Some people make their living solely by renting out rooms or entire houses on Airbnb.

5. Run a social media campaign for a small business.

Many small businesses require a social media manager because they lack the time or skill to publish on social media platforms such as Facebook, Instagram, Snapchat, or Twitter regularly. Take it upon yourself to make contact with local businesses and offer your services for a monthly charge. This is a simple way to earn money regardless of where you reside.

6. Use JustAnswer to answer questions.

JustAnswer and other similar websites pay you to answer professional questions. You may get paid to help others understand certain themes or areas of controversy in life if you have a high-level skill, such as knowledge in law, medical, or information technology.

7. Use Fiverr to sell services.

Fiverr was essential in the emergence of the Gig Economy. Even though services start at $5, some Fiverr vendors earn six figures or more every year. You can sell almost anything on it, but to thrive and become a Super Seller, you must provide tremendous amounts of value, even at lower price points.

8. Use Mechanical Turk to do micro-jobs.

Amazon's Mechanical Turk program is one way to gain money, albeit it will not make you wealthy. However, if you're seeking to do a series of micro-jobs that each takes a few minutes to complete, you could earn some money that could come in handy if you're in a pinch.

9. Teach via Skype.
You can tutor individuals via Skype from anywhere in the world. This is fantastic, especially if you're a digital nomad searching for a way to supplement your income beyond what the local employment market can offer. If you're travelling through Asia or another low-cost-of-living country, tutor folks from the United States or the United Kingdom.

10. Get a part-time job.
Okay, so you're short on cash and already have a full-time job, and you're not sure you'd be comfortable making money online or hustling with a web-based enterprise. You might be able to find part-time work. You can say goodbye to your social life, but it's an additional source of income.

11) Create a blog.
So, a blog isn't going to make you rich overnight. However, if you create a blog and provide a lot of value, you can set yourself up with a platform for generating a lot of passive income. You can easily grow this on the side with just a few hours of work per week, but you must regularly produce outstanding content.

12. Create an online course.

You may generate a significant side money stream by building courses that give huge levels of value, depending on how much time you invest in your course.

13. Produce an audiobook.

Create audiobooks and sell them on apps like Audible and iTunes using a platform like ACX. With the correct volume of audiobooks, you can easily produce a five-figure monthly income if you have a brilliant idea for a non-fiction audiobook to teach tough skills like stock trading, foreign currency investing, accounting, web marketing, or others.

14. Become a personal chef.

Are you a talented chef? You may work as a personal chef, preparing meals for others. You might easily sell your services on social media or even develop a website from scratch. There are numerous websites where you can advertise your services, such as HireAChef.

15. Walk dogs.

Dog walking is a skill that almost everyone can learn. Create a few fliers on your computer and place them in mailboxes if you live in a dog-friendly community. Indicate that you are a dog walker and offer a price. Build up a constant supply of customers, and your dog-walking business will flourish.

16. Babysit or become a nanny.

You could always start babysitting or even become a part-time nanny if you need some extra cash. You may do this on a variety of websites, such as Care.com or SitterCity, or you can even advertise your services on social media sites. You'll be vetted and graded for your services, so make sure you deliver a great one.

17. Clean houses.

There's always the option of hiring housekeeping. Many private families and homeowners rent their properties out on a short-term basis and require housekeeping or cleaning services. To promote yourself, you can list your services on sites like HouseKeeper.com and others.

18. Participate in market research focus groups.

Marketing firms frequently hold focus groups to investigate consumer reactions to products, services, and advertisements across various channels. It does not necessitate any specific training.

19. Have a garage sale.

You could always have a garage sale to raise money while getting rid of unwanted items in your home. This is ideal if you have children who have outgrown their toys or if you simply have a huge amount of goods to get rid of. Place some signs around town or use Craigslist to advertise.

20. Make video tutorials for YouTube.

Although it isn't the quickest option to make money on the side, creating YouTube lessons can help you earn a reasonable amount of money if you produce interesting content that keeps people interested for long enough. You can also utilize free tutorials to upsell visitors on the items and services you're selling.

The benefits of being your own boss

Although most people with "regular" jobs want to know what it's like to be their own boss, any rational person would recognize that self-employment is likely to be fraught with difficulties. Not everyone has "what it takes" to start and run a successful business, but if you believe you are creative, persistent, and resourceful enough to make a good livelihood as the CEO of your firm, consider the following ten benefits of being your boss over working for someone else:

1. Greater Control

As a self-employed business owner, you'll have the power to make executive decisions that will impact not just the future of your company but also the future of your family and career. You can only exercise control as an employee within the parameters of your job description.

2. Flexible Work Hours

The freedom to pick when you want to work is one of the most tempting sorts of control an entrepreneur enjoys. Working erratic hours and failing to stick to a set work schedule, on the other hand, is a surefire method to sabotage your company's success. Be realistic and don't take too many holidays; otherwise, your progress will suffer. Remember that balancing work and life is an important part of becoming a successful business owner.

3. Open-Ended Career Progression

As an employee, your chances of being promoted to a more profitable position are restricted. Pay hikes are extremely infrequent, and when they do occur, they are often minor. On the contrary side, your earning potential is only limited by your determination and ability as a self-employed person. If you choose to take this road, you can leverage the plaudits you've earned as the manager/CEO of your firm to seek similar employment opportunities with larger firms in the future.

4. Greater Sense of Satisfaction

When you perform a good job as an employee, you may be recognized with an "employee of the month" certificate, a minor pay raise that very marginally boosts your hourly rate, or even a simple "pat on the back" from superiors during a company meeting. When you continuously perform effectively as a self-employed business owner, however, your entire company benefits, your income progressively improves, and you feel a far larger feeling of satisfaction and fulfillment as a result.

5. Diverse Learning Experience

You'll acquire essential lessons in accounting, micromanagement, consumer psychology, raising productivity, handling professional communication, and countless other topics linked to business management as you progress as a young entrepreneur. This expertise will be valuable regardless of whether you decide to return to work for another company or pursue the more entrepreneurial path of starting new businesses.

6. Forming Positive Habits and Attributes

If a self-employed individual wants to create enough revenue to meet personal and company financial commitments, he or she must acquire certain habits and tendencies. You are the only person that is standing in the way of your success as your boss. Long-term business owners and operators develop timeliness, diplomacy, reliability, diligence, and frugality. You're never compelled to embrace such attributes as an employee of another company because you don't have the same level of responsibility as a self-employed person.

7. Enhanced Business Networking

Unless you work for another company in advertising, marketing, or public relations, odds are you'll conduct more networking as the owner of your own company. You'll almost certainly have to connect and deal with people in adjacent industries frequently to market and operate your business properly. As a result, you'll likely have more opportunities to meet other business owners and managers, increasing the number of networking possibilities available to you.

8. Higher Motivation and Morale

When you go to work every day and do the same activities for a predetermined pay or income, things might get a little boring; however, the degree of spontaneity involved in running a business on your own allows for a lot more excitement and passion. They are also more self-assured and have greater general morale as a result of their financial freedom.

9. Employment Protection

Whether you offer products or services, one reality remains constant: as long as your firm survives in operation, you'll always have a job as the owner/director. On the other hand, an employee may or may not work for their current employer from one year to the next. Even if your firm experiences difficulties and income declines, as a self-employed individual, you will still be able to commence recovery and take control of the situation.

10. The Ability to Retire Sooner

Last but not least, self-employment retirement plans allow you to save more for retirement since you can make bigger annual contributions to your solo 401(k) account than you could with an employer-sponsored retirement plan (which would have more restrictive maximum contribution limits). Self-employment gives you additional options to create the type of money needed to pay an early retirement, in addition to allowing you to contribute more to your retirement account each year.

Why You Will Eventually want to Quit Your Job to Become Your Boss

Like an indecisive pendulum, you swing back and forth. Is it true that I should leave? Perhaps it isn't so horrible. Maybe if I only wait a little longer, things will improve. You will consider several factors when deciding whether or not to leave a job.

- You don't aspire to be a higher-ranking official - If you are not motivated enough to progress or get promoted to a higher rank or level, it might be the time that you should leave the job.
- Your workplace is toxic - If you are always being criticized or not being valued enough, this might be the time to consider leaving the job.
- You have little control over your life - If you always feel exhausted and have no or little control over your life, you definitely need to switch job because a job is a part of life, don't make it your whole life.
- You have a cash emergency reserve - If you have a certain amount of cash reserved for you, you should definitely leave

a job and think of investing your money in something more beneficial.

- Your job no longer aligns with your ideals - If your job doesn't match your life goals, you better quit the job and find something worth it.
- You want to start a business - This is the most common reason why most people prefer quitting a 9 to 5 job. If you have an idea, don't wait and build your own business.
- You've gotten as far as you want to go - Some people quit a job when they think they have earned enough to live the rest of their lives at peace or have reached a level where they don't want anything anymore.
- The term "additional project" makes you cry - People usually get exhausted when they have to wear many caps in an organization. They resign from their position as they do not enjoy doing any additional work except for their job.
- You despise Mondays more than a smear test - It's a clear sign that you want to quit your job if you hate and fear Mondays more than anything. You are continuously waiting for the weekends, so you don't have to go to work.
- You've given up on impressing your superiors - When there is no desire left in you to impress your seniors or superiors, it is a sign that you are not into your job anymore and need a quick change.
- Your job responsibilities have grown, but your income has not - Most people quit their jobs when they feel like they are not

being paid enough according to the duties or roles they are assigned.

- You spend hours on Instagram looking at travel photographs - You need to leave a job when you hardly get time to enjoy life or travel, and you spend most of your time looking at travel photos and wishing you could be there.
- You only talk about how much you despise your job - When you only talk about how negative your job is, and you don't find even a single good thing to talk about, that's when you are mentally done with your job.
- You've lost faith in your industry - At a certain stage, people realize that the industry or company they work for only cares about themselves and not about its employees and end up leaving the job.

How to increase your network

Everyone understands that the breadth and depth of one's professional network are critical to one's success, yet we frequently take a passive approach and expect our network to grow on its own with no effort on our part. It's also easy to conflate mindless social media scrolling at lunch with actively expanding our professional network. They aren't the same thing. Professionals with strong networks work hard to maintain them, so don't make the mistake of becoming complacent and allowing your network to stagnate (or worse). Develop a precise goal to expand your professional network before the first month of the year passes you by. Discussed below are a few suggestions to help you increase your network.

Tip #1: Strengthen existing bonds.
Quality might be just as essential as quantity when it comes to expanding your professional network (if not more). Instead of focusing just on increasing your contact list, think about how you might strengthen the ones you already have. Don't wait until you're in a pinch to reach out to a valuable connection you've recently made. When you don't need anything, purposefully reach out to a coworker or new acquaintance.

Tip #2: Schedule a monthly networking lunch to expand your network.
Without a doubt, the greatest moment to establish a relationship with a senior leader or subject matter expert is before you want their assistance. The unfortunate reality is that we typically wait until a crisis occurs before desperately trying to find someone who knows the person we want to influence, which can lead to less-than-ideal outcomes. Trying to create a relationship amid a crisis rarely works out. Create a monthly calendar of relationship-building lunches or coffees instead. It may not sound enticing today, but you'll be pleased you did it in a year. It's a piece of cake.

The Career Change Quest

Tip #3: Increase your LinkedIn activity.

Undoubtedly, LinkedIn is one of the most significant social networking sites for business professionals, and if you aren't using it, you're likely missing out on opportunities to connect with people who can help you (or who can assist you) this year, next year, or ten years from now. No, you are not required to post many times every day or to remark on as many posts as possible at random. Keep in mind that increasing your network by 20% with quality connections is likely to be more advantageous than increasing it by 40% with random connections.

Tip #4: Expand your horizons by learning something new.

Part of our networks become stagnant because it's so natural to concentrate nearly entirely on our area of expertise. While it's crucial to focus on your functional area, you may be unknowingly limiting yourself by failing to explore alternative possibilities. Stepping out of one's comfort zone is important for broadening your skill set and expanding your professional network. By dipping your toe into the water of other professional specialties, you'll gain access to a whole new group of contacts and connections.

Tip #5: Set up a meeting with your manager early in the year to get consent to attend your chosen conferences/training events.

Conferences and training events allow you to broaden your intellect as well as your network. Most professionals recognize the value of attending training/conferences, but they frequently make the error of waiting until the last minute to request approval. When you ask early in the year, you have a better chance of getting the money before budgets get too tight.

Tip #6: Send people stuff

It isn't as hard as you think. You have to provide value to people, curate material, bring inspiration and knowledge. No, I don't mean sending them any commercial fluff. Instead, send them material that has been of great interest to you and will be useful for them using your knowledge of the individual with whom you are attempting to network. Let me offer you a handy example. You can provide quality-related content such as articles, videos, blog posts, etc. If you know that a close network is working on a project, and you are sitting on content that could benefit them, don't hesitate to provide that value. The way the human mind functions is to treat every gift or favour, which must be reciprocated. I recommend you to do this process maximum of once a week. This is to avoid it becoming "obvious" or "badgering". You want to be choiceful about what you send to make sure that it is valuable and not harassing people. Remember, provide value first, without expecting anything in return. Build up that value equity with your network first, and when the day comes where you are in need of a favour, they will be more likely to return it.

CHAPTER 9

START YOUR BUSINESS IN 2021

How to start a business in 2021

In today's competitive world, having a strong business idea is no longer enough to be successful. Whether you're starting an online business or intending to open a physical location, there are a few things to keep in mind to build a competitive business in 2021.

1. Find the Right Market to Target

The main goal of any new entrepreneur should be to present their services/products to a rapidly increasing or well-developed market. Competition is fierce in popular fields, making your task even more difficult. To stand out in a large crowd, you must establish a competitive advantage. This mostly consists of three elements:

- Service quality and innovation
- The ideal pricing point
- Outstanding Customer service

To distinguish yourself from the crowd, your target audience will naturally anticipate certain things from you. You can only reach the correct individuals if you conduct market research and learn what they want before developing your plans. Gather as much information as possible about your target market and build your business plan on your findings.

2. Get the Right People by Your Side

Individuals do not build great brands; teams do. Even though you are the owner and leader of a company, you must recognize that you will require the assistance of others. You need the appropriate people on your side to establish a firm from the ground up, whether they be employees, partners, managers, friends, or family. Learn what you'll need to get your business off the ground before you start it. What kind of experts do you require? Are you able to obtain the information you require on your own, or do you require the assistance of research experts? Do you need to hire a professional to write your business plan or do it yourself?

Consider competent workers, motivational leaders, training opportunities, salespeople and managers, accounting firms, marketing specialists, and legal aid, among other things. Even if you are an industry specialist, there will be times when you require assistance.

3. Create a Solution

Rather than worrying about what you'll sell or how much money you'll make, concentrate on what you can do for your target market. It will be easier for you to expand your customer base as a result of this. Putting yourself in your customers' shoes will reveal exactly what to provide, how to deliver it, and who to target. Your company should provide a solution rather than merely a wide offer to everybody who stumbles across it. People typically purchase items because they require them. Most of your consumers will have an issue that your firm can solve, so call it an itch that needs scratching. They're looking for a solution, and if you provide one, they'll immediately choose your brand.

Before you begin, consider the following three considerations:

- What issues does your buyer persona require resolution?
- What types of challenges can you address, and how do you go about doing so?
- What are the advantages of patronizing your new company?

Your greatest strategy right now is to figure out what this itch is for your target audience. All of your strategies and advertising can be based on delivering a solution to a problem. Just make sure that your organization is solely focused on solving a problem in 2021.

4. Take Care of Your Financing

The majority of new firms are now financed by the owners' savings or bank loans. Nowadays, starting a business is costly, especially if you haven't budgeted for it. If you go into this blindly, you'll run into a slew of unforeseen costs that will put a stop to your progress before you even get a chance to shine on the market. When you're starting a business, you'll need money. Today's expenses are limitless. You'll need to pay personnel, find a business location, engage marketing gurus, lawyers, and pay for social media advertising, among other things.

As a result, create a specific, extremely detailed financial plan for your new business. Try to plan ahead of time and budget for certain unplanned expenses. You should begin this trip only when you are confident that you will cover your business expenses until it begins to make money.

5. Consider SEO.

For many years, SEO has been popular. Every year, it evolves and becomes more and more significant. This should be at the top of your priority list if you're launching a business in 2021. Today, most organizations need an online presence, and it can help them grow faster than any other method. Google's method of deciding whether or not your site deserves to rank higher for search engine queries is called SEO, or Search Engine Organization. Your business will not reach the target audience you intended if it has a bad web presence and poor SEO. Before you start your new business, now is the time to explore SEO tactics. Even if you succeed and things go well for you, you must keep up with the latest SEO trends. Algorithms and expectations vary daily, so be sure your strategy is geared toward achieving higher rankings.

6. Leverage the power of social media

Many individuals use social media sites like Facebook and Instagram to find the services and goods they need, making social media an important aspect of any modern business strategy. This necessitates the usage of social media by new businesses to reach out and target a larger audience. This is a method for establishing your brand, attracting new consumers, converting leads, and communicating with your buyer persona.

The following are some of the most recent business social media strategies:

- Set defined objectives and goals for social media networks.
- Investigate your competitors via social media.
- Look for ideas on many platforms.
- Make a social media calendar that you will adhere to.
- Make a plan to be present on several platforms.
- Find the best platforms, posting times, and social media groups for your business.

7. Offer outstanding customer service.

Customers nowadays have high expectations in terms of customer service. Their expectations are rising and changing all the time, so if you want your business to prosper, you need to enhance your support service and keep up with the latest trends. Customer service has never been more necessary or valued than it is now, thanks to the worldwide health crisis of 2020. Now, businesspeople must show that they care about their clients by providing them with the services they require professionally and timely. Customer expectations are higher than ever, compared to the past when customer service was mediocre at best and consumers were content with it. The majority of customers want businesses to provide support 24 hours a day, seven days a week. If and when they have inquiries, they are not willing to wait for a response.

Customer service issues may ruin a brand before it even gets off the ground. Even if they offered valuable items and services, over 80% of customers abandon a brand and write negative reviews because of poor customer service. Even so, most businesses these days do not provide quick responses or good customer service. As a young entrepreneur, you should take advantage of this. People who are dissatisfied with the speed with which your competitors provide replies and solutions will call you. If you can provide them with excellent customer service, they will be significantly more inclined to choose you and spread the word about your company.

Why having a 9-5 job is riskier than you think

A 9-5 job was a popular option since it provided a sense of security. You'd probably be ok if you did your job and didn't offend any upper management with your actions.

If your workplace becomes toxic, you may begin looking for a new job ahead of time and make the shift gradually. Your previous work experience served as a safety net. Hiring managers and recruiters would be pleased if you spent several years at the same company and had a consistent industry theme on your resume.

Norms are currently being thrown out the window. People in the workforce who are in charge of hiring are swamped with applications, which might endure for years.

These people will be victorious.

Those who become more creative will benefit from the shift in risk profile associated with 9-5 work. People having two or more revenue streams based on a growing number of relevant talents will be the winners. Skills that are centered on digital products and services will be in high demand. We owe it to ourselves to broaden our professional horizons.

Your savior will be a financial buffer.

After this crisis passes, there will be numerous false starts. It must be a great blessing to be able to sit on the sidelines with a small sum of money. You will have bought yourself time and peace of mind if you saved during the good times and practiced for the hard times. There are countless false starts when the planet undergoes massive economic resets. The worst may appear to have passed, only for the economic problem to take on a new dimension that no one anticipated. You don't have to try to foresee what will happen if you rely on your financial buffer, sometimes known as cash in the bank. It's never a bad idea to have a financial cushion on hand.

A hobby can help you to reduce the risk even further.

Hobbies can help you avoid danger. They provide you the opportunity to exercise your creative freedom and question yourself, "Could I maybe generate money from this in the future?" That one question has the potential to change your life. Develop your interests and convert them into mini-empires. When you have free time, practice your passion and charge a small fee where you can while simultaneously improving their skill level.

Innovative Businesses Will Succeed

Employees who have picked firms that do not innovate will be the ones who suffer the most. They're the businesses that hold twenty meetings to decide whether or not to publish a blog post and consult the IT department before making any decisions. Workers in creative organizations are all familiar with how to make decisions in the digital economy. Innovative businesses use a large number of IT professionals rather than relying on a single department. These are the businesses that will be less vulnerable in the new economy.

People will continue to work 9-5 jobs. The most important thing to understand is that 9-5 employment is no longer a secure haven. When the economy collapses, and leaders with a bird's-eye view of the globe are compelled to fire people or face being dismissed, there won't be time to meet with you and hear your opinion.

Common setbacks faced by start-ups

You can prepare accordingly and offer yourself the best chance of success if you understand the major reasons why most businesses fail. This data can guide you in determining which industries and demographics to target and which pitfalls to avoid. Above all, it might inspire you to believe that where there is a will, there is a way.

Small Business Failure Statistics

- Small enterprises only make it through the first-year 78.5 percent of the time.
- Entrepreneurs beyond the age of 30 are more likely to fail.
- The most typical cause for small businesses failing is that their products or services are simply not in demand.

- Businesses that run out of funds account for 29% of all failures.
- Only 17% of restaurants fail in their first year of operation.

Small enterprises only make it through the first-year 78.5 percent of the time.

New beginnings are difficult for anyone, but especially for businesses. The journey ends for 21.5 percent of small enterprises before the first year is up. Only approximately half of companies survive the fifth fiscal year. And there aren't many companies that can say they've been in business for a decade.

According to statistics, barely one-third of all entrepreneurs live to see their tenth birthday.

Since 1977, the failure rate of small businesses has decreased by 30%.

If our first statistic was depressing, we hope this data on small business success rates will lift your spirits. The best part is that your chances of starting a successful business are now 30% higher than they were in the late 1970s. According to Scott Shane, a university lecturer, this increasing success can be attributed to smarter business owners. Indeed, today's entrepreneurs have access to a greater number of resources from which to learn. It's also easier for them to communicate with other business owners and form synergistic business alliances.

The main difficulty for 33% of small business owners is a lack of finance.

According to statistics on small business failure, about a third of business owners believe they don't have enough cash flow to keep their company afloat. Finding a consistent revenue stream and dependable consumers is challenging, and failure to do so frequently forces businesses to close their doors.

Aside from cash flow, which can be improved by judicious use of business loans (for example, this organization offers many types of business loans), entrepreneurs also have marketing issues, time management issues, recruiting obstacles, and administrative work on their minds.

Entrepreneurs beyond the age of 30 are more likely to fail.

Several things determine the success or failure of a business. One of them is experience. According to statistics on small business failure, entrepreneurs over the age of 30 have a somewhat better probability of success. When you look at the high achievers in the top 0.1 percent growth category, you can see how important age is. Only 0.09 percent of business owners under the age of 30 achieve these heights, compared to 0.17 percent of business owners beyond 30. Experience appears to be the deciding factor in this scenario.

Only 17% of restaurants fail in their first year of operation.

For many Americans, owning and operating a restaurant appears to be an unachievable goal doomed from the start. That's because statistics on small business restaurant failure rates abound on the internet, claiming that at least 90% of restaurants fail in their first year. As this study demonstrates, nothing could be further from the truth. In fact, 83% of full-service restaurant businesses survive one year, with a median lifespan of 4.5 years.

Why do Business Fail?

Starting a business is difficult, and numerous statistics on the survival rate of beginning enterprises are available. Entrepreneurship is not for the faint of heart; it is intrinsically dangerous. Successful business owners must manage company-specific risks while also bringing a product or service to market at a price that matches customer demand. To protect a new or existing business, it's important to understand what can cause it to fail and how each obstacle can be controlled or avoided entirely. Small firms fail for various reasons, including a lack of money or finance, the retention of an ineffective management team, a flawed infrastructure or business model, and bad marketing campaigns, among others.

1. Financing Hurdles

Small businesses fail for various reasons, one of which is a lack of money or operating capital. A business owner is usually well aware of how much money is required to keep operations going daily, including funding payroll, paying fixed and variable overhead expenses like rent and utilities, and ensuring that outside vendors are paid on time. On the other hand, owners of failed businesses are less aware of how much revenue is made through product or service sales. This gap causes cash problems, which can put a small business out of business quickly.

Small businesses in the early stages of development may have difficulty securing funding to launch a new product, expand, or cover continuing marketing expenses. While angel investors, venture capitalists, and traditional bank loans are among the funding options accessible to small businesses, not every company has the income stream or growth trajectory that qualifies them for large funding. Small firms are compelled to close their doors due to a lack of funds for significant projects or continuing working capital needs.

2. Inadequate Management

A lack of business understanding on the part of the management team or the firm owner is another prevalent factor for small enterprises failing. In some cases, especially when a company is in its initial year or two of existence, a firm owner is the only senior-level employee.

While the owner may have the abilities to develop and market a profitable product or service, they frequently lack the qualities of a good manager and lack time to manage others effectively. A business owner with no dedicated management staff is more likely to mismanage some parts of the firm, such as finances, hiring, or marketing.

3. Poor Business Planning

Prior to opening their doors, many small firms neglect the necessity of comprehensive business planning. At the very least, a good business strategy should include:

- A detailed explanation of the company
- Employee and management requirements now and in the future
- Opportunities and threats within the broader market
- Capital requirements, including cash flow projections and multiple budgets
- Initiatives in marketing
- Analyzing your competitors

Before operations begin, business owners who fail to meet the company's demands through a well-thought-out plan set their organizations up for major problems. Similarly, a company that does not examine its initial business plan regularly — or is not prepared to adjust to changes in the market or industry — will face insurmountable challenges during the course of its existence.

4. Mistakes in Marketing

Many business owners fail to plan for their company's marketing needs regarding finance, prospect reach, and precise conversion ratio estimates. It can be really challenging to get funding or redirect cash from other corporate units to cover the difference when organizations misjudge the entire cost of early marketing initiatives. Because marketing is such an important component of any early-stage organization, organizations must ensure that they have set reasonable marketing budgets for present and future needs.

Similarly, establishing realistic forecasts for target audience reach and sales conversion ratios is crucial to the success of a marketing campaign. Businesses that do not grasp these characteristics of effective marketing strategies are more likely to fail than those that take the time to develop and conduct cost-efficient, successful campaigns.

My final request…
Being a smaller author, reviews help me tremendously!
It would mean the world to me if you could leave a review.

Customer reviews

⭐⭐⭐⭐⭐ 5 out of 5

12 customer ratings

5 star	▇▇▇▇▇▇▇▇	100%
4 star		0%
3 star		0%
2 star		0%
1 star		0%

˅ How does Amazon calculate star ratings?

Review this product

Share your thoughts with other customers

[Write a customer review]

If you liked reading this book and learned a thing or two, please let me know!

It only takes 30 seconds but means so much to me!

Thank you and I can't wait to see your thought

Conclusion

Pretty sure that this book must have been a great partner in your journey of finding the right career for you. You must have found the answers to each question or doubt that was a hurdle for you in changing your career path. At least, now you have a direction to move forward in order to find happiness and satisfaction in your career.

The ultimate reason for publishing this book was to help anybody stuck in his/her life or unhappy by his/her present career choices. I have tried my level best to explain things in-depth as well as keeping them precise, so you don't have to waste your energy to get to the point you're actually looking for. It is made sure that each and every question or problem related to career choices has been addressed. Some real-life examples have been presented to inspire you that you are not alone in this, and if they can do it, you can do it too. Finally, a few key tips and hacks have been addressed to assist you obtain stability in this uncertain period of COVID -19.

However, in the end, the most important thing that I would recommend you to take away from this book is your willingness to make your career a happy part of your life as is the common saying 'WHERE THERE IS A WILL THERE'S A WAY' so if you're willing to change your life for good you will definitely do it and even if you fail, giving yourself a chance is a fair move, so you have no regrets that you never tried because the biggest failure is a person who never tried in the first place because of a fear of defeat.

REFERENCES

Black, J. (2021). *In my job search, how do I assess which roles fit best?*. Ft.com. Retrieved 17 June 2021, from https://www.ft.com/content/b777b07d-8074-4a61-aca6-716e1cff21e1.

Patel, S. (2017). *The 5 Personality Traits All Entrepreneurs Must Have.* Entrepreneur. Retrieved 17 June 2021, from https://www.entrepreneur.com/article/298650.

18 glaring signs you are ready to quit your job. Medium. (2018). Retrieved 17 June 2021, from https://medium.com/the-ascent/18-glaring-signs-you-are-ready-to-quit-your-job-31d9b446cdbd.

Brownlee, D. (2020). *6 Ways To Boost Your Professional Network In The New Year.* Forbes. Retrieved 17 June 2021, from https://www.forbes.com/sites/danabrownlee/2020/01/02/6-ways-to-boost-your-professional-network-in-the-new-year/?sh=48893fdf6862.

International Labour Organization. (2021). *ILO Monitor: COVID-19 and the world of work. Seventh edition Updated estimates and analysis* (pp. 7-35). International Labour Organization. Retrieved from https://www.ilo.org/wcmsp5/groups/public/@dgreports/@dcomm/documents/briefingnote/wcms_767028.pdf

Saunders, A. >*TECHNOLOGY'S IMPACT ON GROWTH AND EMPLOYMENT* [Ebook] (1st ed., pp. 1-20). OpenMind BBVA. Retrieved 17 June 2021, from https://www.bbvaopenmind.com/wp-content/uploads/2018/03/BBVA-OpenMind-Adam-Saunders-Technologys-Impact-on-Growth-and-Employement.pdf.

Malinsky, G. (2020). *These 15 jobs will be in high demand over the next 5 years — some with salaries topping $80,000.* CNBC.com. Retrieved 17 June 2021, from https://www.cnbc.com/2020/07/20/jobs-growing-in-high-demand-over-next-5-years-some-pay-more-than-80000-in-salary.html.

("Free personality test, type descriptions, relationship and career advice | 16Personalities", n.d.)

Bolles, R., & Brooks, K. (2020). *What Color is Your Parachute?.*

LaPonsie, M. (2021). *25 Best Jobs That Don't Require a College Degree.* money.usnews.com. Retrieved 17 June 2021, from https://money.usnews.com/money/careers/slideshow/25-best-jobs-that-dont-require-a-college-degree?slide=5.

www.ingramcontent.com/pod-product-compliance
Lightning Source LLC
LaVergne TN
LVHW012045070526
838202LV00056B/5597

9 7 8 3 9 8 8 1 7 8 9 0 9